Oxford Read and Discover

Teacher's Handbook

Levels 3–6

Hazel Geatches, Series Editor

Contents

OXFORD
UNIVERSITY PRESS

Great Clarendon Street, Oxford, OX2 6DP, United Kingdom

Oxford University Press is a department of the University of Oxford. It furthers the University's objective of excellence in research, scholarship, and education by publishing worldwide. Oxford is a registered trade mark of Oxford University Press in the UK and in certain other countries

© Oxford University Press 2011

The moral rights of the author have been asserted

First published in 2011
2017 2016
10 9 8 7 6 5 4 3 2

All rights reserved. No part of this publication may be reproduced, stored in a retrieval system, or transmitted, in any form or by any means, without the prior permission in writing of Oxford University Press, or as expressly permitted by law, by licence or under terms agreed with the appropriate reprographics rights organization. Enquiries concerning reproduction outside the scope of the above should be sent to the ELT Rights Department, Oxford University Press, at the address above

You must not circulate this work in any other form and you must impose this same condition on any acquirer

Links to third party websites are provided by Oxford in good faith and for information only. Oxford disclaims any responsibility for the materials contained in any third party website referenced in this work

Photocopying

The Publisher grants permission for the photocopying of those pages marked 'photocopiable' according to the following conditions. Individual purchasers may make copies for their own use or for use by classes that they teach. School purchasers may make copies for use by staff and students, but this permission does not extend to additional schools or branches

Under no circumstances may any part of this book be photocopied for resale

ISBN: 978 0 19 464375 7

Printed in China

This book is printed on paper from certified and well-managed sources

The Publisher and Series Editor would like to thank John Clegg (CLIL Adviser) and Robert Quinn (Teaching Notes Adviser) for their input.

About Oxford Read and Discover

Oxford Read and Discover is a series of graded Readers from Levels 1 to 6, suitable for students of English from age six and older. The levels have been designed to match the language content of Elementary English language coursebooks from Grades 1 to 6.

These reading books provide a wide variety of non-fiction topics that can be used for cross-curricular work or for Content and Language Integrated Learning (CLIL). The topics have been chosen to stimulate students' interest and to cover key curriculum content from three broad subject areas: The World of Science and Technology, The Natural World, and The World of Arts and Social Studies.

Oxford Read and Discover combines lively reading material with carefully graded language, enabling students to discover more about the world while learning English at the same time. See the series chart on the back cover and the contents summary chart on pages 4–5. Or go to **www.oup.com/elt/teacher/readanddiscover**

Series Components, Levels 3–6

Reader

Each Reader provides carefully structured and supported **reading text** about an engaging topic. The following features support the development of general reading skills.

- The **contents page** and **introduction page** at the beginning of the Reader prepare students for what they will read in the chapters.
- The **reading text** is organized into **chapters**, each with a **heading**. In Levels 5 and 6, there is also **introductory text** for each chapter, and the chapters are organized into short sections with **sub-headings**. The text is accompanied by **photos**, **illustrations**, and **diagrams**, to stimulate interest and support understanding, and **labels** are included for key language and concepts. There are also **Discover! fact boxes** and **cartoons**, to further stimulate interest.

At the back of each Reader the following are provided.

- Two pages of **activities** for each chapter. These activities are carefully graded and are based on the language and content of the chapter. They are designed to support the development of a range of reading and writing skills, as well as general cognitive skills and critical thinking skills. The activities can be done after each chapter, or after the whole Reader has been read.
- Two **projects** that provide extension material, encouraging students to personalize the topic, share their ideas with others, or research the topic further. Structured support is provided for these activities.
- To support the development of dictionary skills, in Levels 3 and 4 there is a **picture dictionary** for key vocabulary that is likely to be new. In Levels 5 and 6 a **glossary** with simple definitions is provided instead.

Audio CD

An Audio CD accompanies each Reader, and provides a recording of the text in both American and British English.

Activity Book

An Activity Book is available for each Reader, providing additional reading, writing, and grammar practice for each chapter, as well as consolidation activities, and a book review page. Activity Book answers are available on the Teacher's Website at **www.oup.com/elt/teacher/readanddiscover**

Teacher's Handbook Levels 3–6

This Teacher's Handbook outlines the methodology of the **Oxford Read and Discover** series, and provides an **overview** of the Readers at levels 3–6, to help with lesson planning. There are **general teaching suggestions** that you can adapt to specific Readers and teaching contexts, and there are some ideas on using the **photocopiable world map** provided on page 7. **CLIL guidance notes** are also provided on page 8.

There is a page of **specific teaching notes** for each Reader, providing a summary of topics, curriculum links, main vocabulary and grammar, as well as **answers** to the Reader activities. **Specific teaching ideas** are also provided, including opportunities for speaking practice. Look out for the READ & TALK ideas!

Teacher's Website

This Teacher's Handbook and the Activity Book answers are available on the Teacher's Website at **www.oup.com/elt/teacher/readanddiscover**

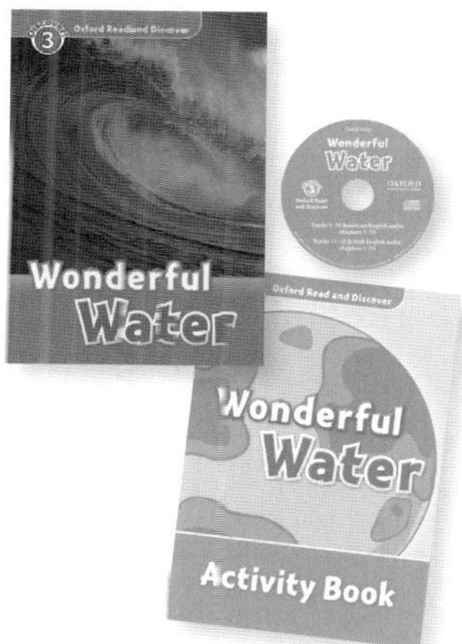

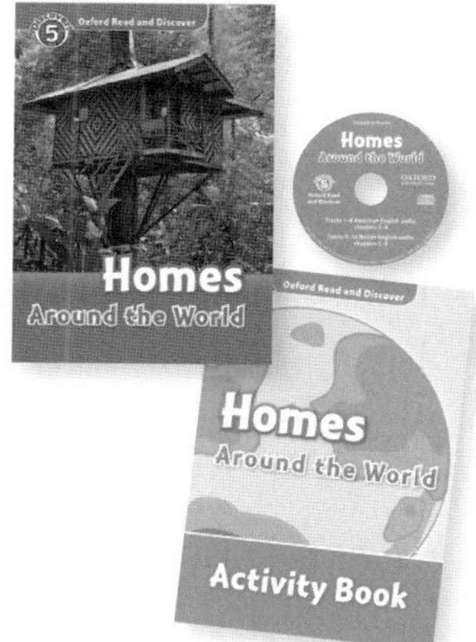

Oxford Read and Discover • Contents Summary, Levels 3–6

Level	Subject Area	Reader Title	Main Vocabulary (For full list see teaching notes for each Reader)	Grammar	Main Topics (For full list see teaching notes for each Reader)	Curriculum Links
3	The World of Science & Technology	How We Make Products	products; materials; machines; clothes; parts of a car; food; parts of the body; buildings	present simple; past simple; question forms; imperative; adjectives; prepositions; adverbs	materials and products; energy and natural resources; tools and machines; industrial processes; parts of a car; food; buildings and construction; art, waste; quantities; sizes and measurements	Art; Civics; Geography; Mathematics; Science; Technology
		Sound and Music	musical instruments; parts of the body; products; animals; transportation; machines; numbers; measurements	present simple/continuous; past simple; question forms; imperative; adjectives; prepositions; adverbs	types of sound; sound waves; how the human voice works; musical instruments; rhythm; recording music; machines; countries	Geography; Music; Mathematics; Science; Technology
		Super Structures	materials; structures; buildings; shapes; transportation; weather; animals; measurements	present simple; past simple; question forms; adjectives; prepositions; adverbs	materials and components; structures in the environment; sizes and measurements; shapes; architecture; places and countries; dates and events; structures made by animals	Art; Geography History; Mathematics; Science; Technology
		Your Five Senses	senses; human body; daily activities; hobbies; musical instruments; food; animals; numbers	present simple/continuous; question forms; adjectives; prepositions; adverbs	human body and senses; light and sound; daily life; disabilities; keeping safe; machines; animals; food	Civics; Mathematics; Music; Science; Technology
	The Natural World	Amazing Minibeasts	minibeasts; other animals; parts of the body; senses; food; plants; numbers; places	present simple; question forms; adjectives; prepositions	classification; life cycles; minibeasts in the environment; senses; parts of the body; plants and pollination; quantities and measurements	Geography; Mathematics; Science
		Animals in the Air	animals; parts of the body; animal movements; plants; places; numbers; measurements; countries	present simple/continuous; past simple; question forms; imperative; adjectives; prepositions; adverbs	animals; animal classification; parts of the body; how animals move; animal homes; food; weather and climate; sizes and measurements	Mathematics; Science
		Life in Rainforests	plants; animals; weather; food; materials; parts of the body; transportation; measurements	present simple/continuous; question forms; imperative; adjectives; prepositions; adverbs	tropical rainforests and the environment; tropical rainforests around the world; animal habitats; rainforest plants; weather; food; rivers; tropical rainforests in danger	Civics; Geography; Mathematics; Science
		Wonderful Water	sources of water; forms of water; seas, and oceans; water cycle; weather; washing at home; animals; human body	present simple; question forms; imperative; adjectives; prepositions	water and the environment; forms of water; water around the world; saving water; floods and droughts; plants and animals; human body; life at home	Civics; Geography; Mathematics; Science
	The World of Arts & Social Studies	Festivals Around the World	months; seasons; family; clothes; weather; food; plants; animals	present simple; past simple; question forms; imperative; adjectives; prepositions; adverbs	dates and events; life at home; traditional celebrations; places and countries; food; clothes and costumes; seasons, weather, and climate; quantities	Civics; Geography; History; Mathematics; Science
		Free Time Around the World	sports; hobbies; weather; transportation; clothes; parts of the body; musical instruments; numbers	present simple; past simple; question forms; adjectives; prepositions	sports and other free-time activities; countries; climate and the environment; musical instruments; quantities and measurements	Civics; Geography; Mathematics; Music
4	The World of Science & Technology	All About Plants	plants; plant parts; food; weather; places; animals; materials; numbers	present simple/continuous; past simple; question forms; imperative; adjectives; prepositions adverbs	plant classification; plant parts; a plant life cycle; photosynthesis; plants in the environment; plants in danger; animals; plant materials	Civics; Geography; History; Mathematics; Science; Technology
		How to Stay Healthy	food and drink; sports; activities; parts of the body; transportation; numbers; measurements; places	present simple/continuous; past simple; question forms; imperative; adjectives; prepositions adverbs	human body; how the body works; healthy food and drink; food types; sports and exercise; life at home; healthy lifestyle; protecting your body	Civics; Geography; Mathematics; Science
		Machines Then and Now	machines; tools; materials; transportation; buildings; weather; fuel; computer parts	present simple; past simple; future simple; question forms; adjectives; prepositions; adverbs	materials and components; machines in the environment; machines that help people; sizes and measurements; energy and fuel; places and countries; dates and events	Civics; Geography; History; Mathematics; Science; Technology
		Why We Recycle	materials; everyday objects; food; numbers; measurements; places	present simple/continuous; question forms; imperative; adjectives; prepositions; adverbs	materials and products; recycling waste; pollution; dangers for the environment; life at home; protecting the environment; quantities and measurements	Civics; Geography; Mathematics; Science; Technology
	The Natural World	All About Desert Life	plants; animals; food; materials; homes; weather; seasons; transportation	present simple/continuous; past simple; question forms; imperative; adjectives; prepositions; adverbs	deserts and the environment; deserts around the world; plants and animals; life at home; seasons, weather, and climate; places and countries; desertification; quantities and measurements	Civics; Geography; Mathematics; Science
		All About Ocean Life	oceans; animals; plants; places; food; parts of the body; numbers; seasons	present simple/continuous; past simple; question forms; adjectives; prepositions; adverbs	oceans and the environment; oceans around the world; plants and animals; food chains; classification; parts of the body; sizes and measurements	Civics; Geography; Science; Mathematics
		Animals at Night	mammals, fish, minibeasts, birds; parts of the body; senses; food; weather; numbers; measurements; places	present simple/continuous; question forms; imperative; adjectives; prepositions; adverbs	animals; animals senses; parts of the body; places and environments; animal migrations; quantities and measurements	Geography; Mathematics; Science
		Incredible Earth	places; materials; animals; weather; transportation; numbers; measurements; countries	present simple/continuous; past simple; question forms; adjectives; prepositions; adverbs	environments around the world; places and countries; sizes and measurements; dates and events; physical processes; animals; dangers from the environment	Civics; Geography; History; Mathematics; Science
	The World of Arts & Social Studies	Animals in Art	animals; colors; parts of the body; senses; shapes; materials; numbers; measurements	present simple/continuous; past simple; question forms; imperative; adjectives; prepositions; adverbs	paintings, drawings, sculptures, and other types of art; colors and shapes; materials; animals; parts of the body; places and countries; dates and events; quantities and measurements	Art; Geography; History; Science; Technology
		Wonders of the Past	buildings; materials; places; animals; hobbies; transportation; measurements; dates	present simple; past simple; question forms; adjectives; prepositions; adverbs	types of building; materials; places and countries; sizes and measurements; dates and events; architecture; sports and other hobbies; animals	Art; Civics; Geography; History; Mathematics; Science; Technology

Subject Area	Reader Title	Main Vocabulary For full list see teaching notes for each Reader	Grammar	Main Topics For full list see teaching notes for each Reader	Curriculum Links
5 The World of Science & Technology	Materials to Products	materials; products; machines; tools; places; buildings; food; clothes	present simple/continuous; past simple; future simple; present perfect; question forms; imperative; passive; adjectives; prepositions; adverbs	materials and products; natural resources; production processes; buildings and construction; shapes; tools and machines; energy and the environment; electronic products	Civics; Geography; History; Mathematics; Science; Technology
	Medicine Then and Now	illnesses; jobs; food; materials; parts of the body; plants; places; buildings	present simple/continuous; past simple; future simple present perfect; question forms; imperative; passive; adjectives; prepositions; adverbs	history of medicine; types of medicine; parts of the body; inside the body; healthy lifestyle; keeping clean; caring for people and curing illnesses; medicines made from plants	Civics; Geography; History; Mathematics; Science; Technology
	Transportation Then and Now	transportation; vehicle parts; materials; fuels; places; weather; animals; measurements	present simple; past simple; present perfect; past continuous; future simple; question forms; passive; adjectives; prepositions; adverbs	transportation; materials and components; how vehicles work; the history of transportation; trade and industry; sizes and measurements; energy, fuel, and the environment; safety	Civics; Geography; History; Mathematics; Science; Technology
	Wild Weather	weather; climates; seasons; places; transportation; energy; measurements; dates	present simple/continuous; past simple; present perfect; future simple; question forms; passive; adjectives; prepositions; adverbs	types of weather; weather, climates, and the environment; changing climates; the water cycle; measurements, speeds, temperatures; energy, fuel, and the environment; places and countries; dates and events	Civics; Geography; History; Mathematics; Science
The Natural World	All About Islands	places; forms of water; plants; animals; parts of the body; food; fruit; transportation	present simple/continuous; past simple; future simple; present perfect; question forms; imperative; passive; adjectives; prepositions; adverbs	types of island; how islands form; places and countries; oceans and continents; plant and animal classification; parts of the body	Civics; Geography; Science
	Animal Life Cycles	animals; parts of the body; places; food; weather; plants; measurements; numbers	present simple; past simple; future simple; question forms; imperative; passive; adjectives; prepositions; adverbs	life cycles; animal classification; parts of the body; animals and their environments; dangers in the environment; protecting animals; quantities and measurements	Civics; Geography; Mathematics; Science
	Exploring Our World	explorers; places; transportation; plants; animals; materials; measurements; dates	present simple/continuous; past simple; present perfect; past continuous; future simple; question forms; passive; adjectives; prepositions; adverbs	explorers and exploring; places and countries; plants and animals; natural resources; physical processes; transportation; directions and orientation; sizes and measurements	Geography; History; Mathematics; Science; Technology
	Great Migrations	animals; parts of the body; places; weather; climate; seasons; plants; buildings	present simple/continuous; past simple; present perfect; future simple; question forms; passive; adjectives; prepositions; adverbs	migrating animals; types of migration; animal life cycles; dangers in the environment; changing climates; protecting animals; places and countries; sizes and measurements	Civics; Geography; Mathematics; Science
The World of Arts & Social Studies	Homes Around the World	homes; rooms; materials; shapes; weather; climates; places; transportation	present simple/continuous; past simple; future simple; question forms; passive; adjectives; prepositions; adverbs	building materials; homes and climates; sizes and measurements; shapes; energy and the environment; poverty and being homeless; countries; dates and events	Civics; Geography; History; Mathematics; Science; Technology
	Our World in Art	types of art; materials; shapes; buildings; weather; animals; plants; fruit	present simple/continuous; past simple; future simple; present perfect; question forms; imperative; passive; adjectives; prepositions; adverbs	types of art; colors, shapes, and perspective; urban and rural landscapes; materials; famous artists; plants and animals; tools and machines; types of light	Art; Civics; Geography; History; Mathematics; Science; Technology
6 The World of Science & Technology	Cells and Microbes	animals; parts of the body; plant parts; food; fuel; places; dates; numbers	present simple; past simple; past continuous; past perfect; question forms; imperative; passive; adjectives; prepositions; adverbs	types of cells and microbes; inside animal cells and plant cells; how cells work; respiration and diffusion; how cells fight infections; keeping clean; cell reproduction	Civics; History; Science
	Clothes Then and Now	clothes; materials; parts of the body; daily activities; weather; seasons; jobs; machines	present simple/continuous; past simple; present perfect; future simple; question forms; imperative; passive; adjectives; prepositions; adverbs	types of clothes; fabrics and materials; the clothing industry; fashion; history of clothes; daily life; local customs; jobs	Art; Civics; Geography; History; Science; Technology
	Incredible Energy	daily activities; products; machines; weather; parts of the body; forms of water; clothes; buildings	present simple/continuous; past simple; future simple; present perfect; question forms; imperative; passive; adjectives; prepositions; adverbs	types of energy; how energy is converted; materials and products; conductors and insulators; tools and machines; plants and animals; natural resources	Science; Technology
	Your Amazing Body	parts of the body; shapes; food; daily activities; sports; diseases; measurements; numbers	present simple; future simple; question forms; imperative; passive; adjectives; prepositions; adverbs	parts of the body; inside the body; cells; how the body works; healthy eating; caring for your body; illness and medicine; sizes and measurements	Civics; Mathematics; Science
The Natural World	All About Space	outer space; planets; places; materials; gases; weather; machines; dates	present simple/continuous; past simple; present perfect; past continuous future simple; question forms; passive; adjectives; prepositions; adverbs	galaxies and stars; solar systems, planets, and moons; quantities, measurements, sizes, temperatures; astronomy; space exploration; machines; materials; countries	Geography; History; Mathematics; Science; Technology
	Caring for Our Planet	natural resources; places; animals; plants; daily routines; food; weather; climate	present simple/continuous; past simple; present perfect; future simple; question forms; passive; adjectives; prepositions; adverbs	the importance of water; conserving energy and natural resources; reducing waste and pollution; dangers in the environment; weather and changing climates; plants and animals; machines, energy, and fuels; transportation	Civics; Geography; History; Science; Technology
	Earth Then and Now	numbers; materials; forms of water; weather; plants; parts of plants; food; seasons	present simple/continuous; past simple; present perfect; question forms; imperative; passive; adjectives; prepositions; adverbs	history of Earth; materials and natural resources; types or rock; the rock cycle; how Earth moves; plants and animals; classification; parts of the body	Civics; Geography; History Mathematics; Science
	Wonderful Ecosystems	plants; animals; parts of the body; places; weather; food; seasons; numbers	present simple/continuous; past simple; future simple; question forms; imperative; passive; adjectives; prepositions; adverbs	types of ecosystem; plants and animals; classification; food chains; parts of the body; weather and changing climates; protecting the environment	Civics; Geography; History; Science
The World of Arts & Social Studies	Food Around the World	fruits and vegetables; dairy products; meat and fish; pulses; nutrients; food production; drinks; typical dishes	present simple past simple; question forms; passive; imperative; adjectives; prepositions; adverbs	food; healthy eating; history of some foods; typical dishes; food festivals; hunger and lack of food; plants and animals; countries	Civics; Geography; History; Science
	Helping Around the World	jobs; school subjects; languages; food; materials; animals; plants; places	present simple/continuous; past simple; future simple; present perfect; past perfect; question forms; imperative; passive; adjectives; prepositions; adverbs	jobs and professions; charities; voluntary work; emergencies; weather and changing climates; caring for plants and animals; protecting the environment	Civics; Geography; Science

Using Oxford Read and Discover Levels 3–6

Oxford Read and Discover is designed to develop reading, writing, listening, and speaking skills, as well as general critical thinking skills. The Readers can be used in a number of ways, with individuals or with a whole class. With a whole class, you have the option of using the same Reader with all students, or allowing your students to read independently, choosing different books at different levels. How you use the Readers will depend on the teaching context and linguistic and cognitive abilities of your students. You can adapt the general teaching suggestions below to suit your needs.

Reading Skills

The main goal of the Readers is to provide opportunities for intensive and extensive reading practice. Students can read intensively, making use of the activities for each chapter at the back of the book as an integrated part of reading. They can do the relevant activities after reading each chapter, or they can do all the activities after finishing the whole Reader.

Students can also use the Readers for extensive practice, reading independently for pleasure. This approach is particularly suitable for students with higher levels of English, or even bilingual students. You may want them to work on Readers in a particular order, or you can allow them to explore the topics in their own order of preference. Encourage students to keep track of the Readers that they have completed.

Writing Skills

The activities at the back of the Reader provide integrated reading and writing practice, with a variety of activity types at word and sentence level, such as labelling, completing sentences, true/false sentences, answering questions, ordering words, correcting sentences, puzzles, and providing personal responses.

The projects provide further opportunities for reading and writing. Students can also do more book- or Internet-based research on a topic, and they can present their findings, for example, as posters, fact boxes, charts, or summaries.

For further reading and writing practice, give students sections of text with key words removed or changed, and ask them to complete or correct the text. You can also give students key words from the picture dictionary or glossary and ask them to write sentences with the words. Students can then create their own versions, and test other students.

The Activity Books provide additional reading and writing practice, including more focus on grammar in Levels 5 and 6.

Listening and Speaking Skills

To develop listening skills, the texts are recorded onto Audio CD. You can choose between American and British English.

	Levels 3 & 4	Levels 5 & 6
American English	tracks 1–10	tracks 1–8
British English	tracks 11–20	tracks 9–16

To raise their awareness of pronunciation and intonation, students can listen to the Audio CD as they read. For active practice of pronunciation and intonation, students can listen and read out loud at the same time, or pause the Audio CD after paragraphs and repeat what they heard. Students can then listen to the Audio CD after they have read each chapter or the whole book, with their books open or closed.

For active listening practice, give students sections of text with key words removed or changed, and ask them to complete or correct the texts while listening.

For speaking practice, use the questions on the introduction page of the Reader (page 3) to engage students in discussion before reading. You can also build on these questions to stimulate discussion after students have read the Reader.

Many of the projects also provide an opportunity to develop listening and speaking skills, for example, with surveys and presentations of research projects. See also the After Reading ideas on page 7, and look out for the READ & TALK ideas in the teaching notes for each Reader.

Critical Thinking Skills

The Readers in this series help to develop critical thinking skills, as students need not only to understand English, but also to process topic information. The activities provide practice of both the language and content of the Reader, and they develop students' critical thinking skills with activities such as organizing information into charts, sequencing or correcting information, solving puzzles, giving personal opinions, writing notes, and planning projects.

Individual Use

If a Reader is read by one student only, the student can work at his/her own pace. You can check their understanding by asking simple questions, for example: *What is your favorite chapter / page / picture? Why?* If the student is also doing the activities, you can check these orally.

Some of the projects ask students to work with others. If a student is not working with a whole class on the same Reader, he/she may be able to talk to other class members in English to do the project. Otherwise he/she can ask friends or members of their family, or you can work with the student.

Whole-Class Use

If a whole class is reading the same Reader, you can use some of the Before Reading and After Reading ideas below and on page 7.

Some projects provide good opportunities for whole-class activities, for example, class surveys. Ideas are provided in the teaching notes for each Reader, and on page 7.

Before Reading

If you are working with the whole class, you can introduce the topic, check on previous knowledge, and stimulate students' interest with the following activities.

- Show the cover, initially hiding the title, and ask students what they think the book is about, and what they already know about the topic, for example: *What is the title of this book? What is this book about? What do you know about…?*
- Ask students what vocabulary they know about the topic, and ask them to guess what vocabulary will be in the Reader. You can write all the vocabulary on the board, and also introduce any key vocabulary from the picture dictionary or glossary that you think students will need. Or you can leave students to find the new vocabulary at the back of the Reader when they need it.
- Use the photos and questions on the introduction page of the Reader (page 3) to stimulate discussion and thought.
- If the Reader includes content from around the world, you can use the ideas and the world map on page 7.
- Before each chapter, ask students about the photos and illustrations. In Levels 5 and 6 you could also read and discuss the introduction text in each new chapter.

After Reading

After each chapter or after the whole Reader has been read, check how much students have understood and provide opportunities for revision and further practice with the following activities as a whole class or in pairs. In a mixed-ability class, students can read at their own pace, and go straight to the activities when they are ready. You can then check students' understanding once they have all finished. If you check answers orally, students can practice their listening skills.

- Say or write sentences about the topic and ask students to say or write if they are true or false.
- Ask or write general comprehension questions.
- Describe something from the Reader without saying its name; ask students to guess what it is, or ask them to ask questions and only answer yes or no.
- Depending on their level, ask students to say or write three, five, or ten new things that they have learned.
- Ask students what their favorite Discover! fact is.
- If students are reading different Readers, ask them to present their Reader to the rest of the class.
- The projects at the back of the Reader provide opportunities for students to do further research, or to personalize the topic. There are also opportunities for whole-class speaking practice, for example, with surveys.
- In Levels 3 and 4, the picture dictionary is a great resource for practice of key vocabulary after reading. Show or say the words and ask students to match them to the pictures, or show the pictures and ask students to say or write the words. In Levels 5 and 6, show or say the glossary definitions, and ask students to write or say the words.

Using the World Map

Oxford Read and Discover provides international, global content, and many of the Readers refer to places all around the world. It is important that students know where key places are, to ensure full understanding of the text. You can use your own maps, atlas, or globe, but to support you and your students, a photocopiable world map is provided below. The map is blank and only shows the continents to provide maximum flexibility – the amount of detail that you or your students add will depend on the Reader, the activity, and the age and level of your students.

Here are some ideas.

- On a copy of the map, mark all the places mentioned in the Reader. Give students a copy of the map to refer to while they read. And/Or after reading, give students a copy of the map and ask them to add information that they have learnt about these places.
- Give students a list of the places mentioned in the Reader and a copy of the blank map. Ask students to mark the places on the map. This can be done as a quiz, or students can use atlases or the Internet. Once the answers have been checked, students refer to the map while they read.
- After reading, give students a copy of the blank map. Ask them to find all the places mentioned in the Reader and to mark them on the map. Then they can add information that they have learned about these places.
- After reading, students can use a copy of the blank map to accompany a presentation of a research project.

Hazel Geatches, Series Editor

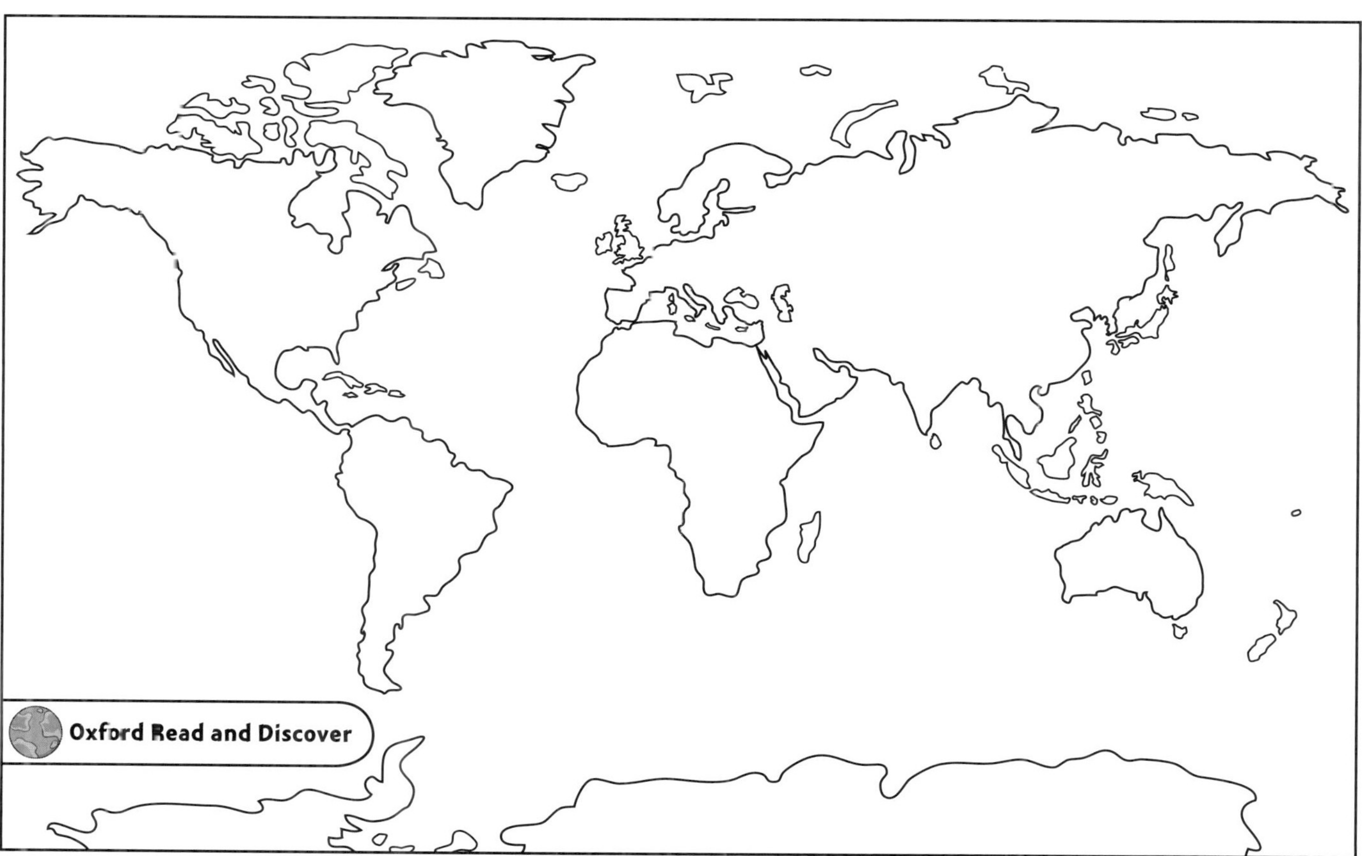

 © Oxford University Press

CLIL Guidance

Learning other subjects through English, or CLIL, is a key feature of the **Oxford Read and Discover** series of graded Readers.

What is CLIL?

CLIL stands for 'Content and Language Integrated Learning' and it links learning subjects with language learning. This helps students to develop both language abilities and subject concepts in the second language. It motivates them to use the language: interesting topics encourage students to read, use, and learn English. Also, CLIL builds on the subject knowledge that students have gained using their first language. Once they have learned about a topic in their first language, it is easier for them to read about it in English; and they can expand their understanding of it in English. To help students to do this, CLIL uses a methodology that makes school subjects accessible to students who may be at an early stage in language learning.

CLIL and Oxford Read and Discover

You can see this methodology at work in the **Oxford Read and Discover** series. The language is carefully graded, plenty of visuals make concepts easy to understand, and the activities are designed to help students to use English and learn about the topic at the same time.

The Readers emphasize reading skills, but they also encourage students to write, talk, and listen to the text or to each other. They highlight vocabulary that is specific to the topic, but they also give students practice in organizing and expressing their ideas and opinions about the topic using simple sentences. They focus on language skills, but also on the skills of thinking and processing information that are required in the study of school subjects, and that the students are developing in their first language.

Because the **Oxford Read and Discover** series combines language with content, the Readers can be used by either subject or language teachers.

For Subject Teachers

Some subject teachers are also English teachers. They like to link the work they do on a subject in the students' first language with their English language lessons. These Readers allow them to do this by reinforcing students' knowledge of specific school topics and developing their English language skills at the same time. Alternatively the subject teacher may collaborate with an English teacher and plan a short coordinated scheme of work on a common topic. The subject teacher leads the teaching of the topic in the first language, and the English teacher reinforces it by using a Reader.

Subject teachers teach a lot of information-processing skills that their subject requires, such as using charts, graphs, and maps, searching for information on the Internet, and presenting information in visual and verbal forms. The **Oxford Read and Discover** series makes use of similar skills; the Readers ask students to construct and interpret graphs and charts, to use the Internet for further investigation of the topics, to do surveys, make notes, plan, and make simple presentations. Subject teachers who also teach English can easily reinforce the information skills they teach in the first language by using these Readers, because they develop the same skills in English. They can also plan collaborative projects with an English teacher, to focus on a common topic, and on common information and learning skills.

For Language Teachers

Many language teachers nowadays like to expand their language teaching to include some work on other subjects in the curriculum. The **Oxford Read and Discover** series helps them to do this by making these topics available to students whose English language ability is still at a developing stage. The graded language of the texts, the visuals, and the supportive activities allow the language teacher to reinforce language development by expanding into a subject, without making inappropriate demands on the English language ability of the students.

The Readers can also reinforce language that the teacher may be focussing on in an English language coursebook, such as specific grammatical structures or vocabulary. The contents summary chart on pages 4–5 shows which aspects of language are highlighted by each Reader. English teachers can choose to link the language work they may be doing in an English language coursebook with a particular Reader that focusses on similar language.

John Clegg, CLIL Adviser

3 How We Make Products

Subject Area
The World of Science & Technology

Topics & Curriculum Links
materials and products (Science; Technology)
energy and natural resources (Science)
tools and machines (Technology)
industrial processes (Technology; Civics)
parts of a car (Technology)
food (Science, Technology)
buildings and construction (Science; Technology)
art, books, and publishing (Art; Technology)
electronic products (Technology)
countries (Geography)
recycling waste (Science; Technology; Civics)
quantities (Mathematics)
sizes and measurements (Mathematics)

Vocabulary
products; materials; machines; clothes; parts of a car; food; parts of the body; buildings; rooms; numbers; measurements; countries

Grammar
present simple; past simple; question forms; imperative; adjectives; prepositions; adverbs

Teaching Ideas

See also pages 6–7 for general ideas that you can adapt. Or go to **www.oup.com/elt/teacher/readanddiscover**

READ & TALK A Product Presentation
After completing Project 1, students present their product to the rest of the class. They can write or talk about their product like this: *This is a ... It's made of ... It's made by hand / in a factory. People make it like this. They ... Then they ... It's used for ...* Posters can then be displayed together.

READ & TALK Which Product Is It?
Choose one of the products from the Reader, and without saying its name, read out one sentence about it and ask students to guess which product it is. Read out more sentences, one at a time, until students guess the correct product. You can use a point scoring system, for example, five points after one fact, three points after two facts, etc. Students can then do this in small groups or pairs.

A Products Display
In small groups, students brainstorm as many products as they can think of and organize them into categories, for example, made by hand/in factories; made of plastic, cotton, wool, plastic, metal; electronic, food, things we wear, transportation. Then they create a display of the products organized into categories, presented as a class mural, or a poster.

Activities Answers

Page 24–25 **1** 1 neck 2 side 3 back 4 strings 5 front **2** 1 hand 2 factories 3 jewelry 4 instruments 5 tools **3** 1 People make guitars from wood 2 They make them by hand. 3 They cut thin pieces of wood. 4 They fix the pieces together with glue. 5 Then they put strings on the guitar. **4** 1 factories 2 string 3 tools 4 front **5** 1 jewelry 2 chairs 3 clocks 4 musical instruments

Page 26–27 **1** 1 cotton 2 fabric 3 pocket 4 buttons 5 zipper 6 wool 7 clothes 8 jeans **2** 1 false 2 true 3 false 4 true 5 true **3** 1 cotton 2 machines 3 needles 4 pieces **4** Jess is wearing a pair of <u>jeans</u>. They are (<u>color</u>) and they're made of <u>cotton</u>. She's also wearing a <u>sweater</u>. It's (<u>color</u>) and it's made of <u>wool</u>. **5** free answers

Page 28–29 **1** 1 mold 2 model 3 toys 4 blow 5 waste 6 recycle **2** 1 people 2 shape 3 store 4 parts 5 bottle 6 machine 7 product 8 plastic **3** 1 People draw a new toy. 2 They make a model of the toy. 3 They make a mold for each part. 4 Machines use hot plastic and molds to make plastic parts. 5 People or machines fix the parts together. **4** free answers

Page 30–31 **1** 1 steel 2 robots 3 seats 4 chassis 5 door **2** 1 parts 2 moves things 3 chassis 4 machines 5 can **3** 1 chassis 2 shapes 3 robots 4 conveyor 5 parts 6 paint 7 wheels **4** 1 A car chassis is made of steel. 2 There are about 35,000 parts. 3 They make 48 million cars. 4 They can recycle the steel.

Page 32–33 **1** 1 dough 2 noodles 3 fingers 4 flour **2** 1 chocolate bars 2 noodles 3 chocolate bars 4 chocolate bars 5 noodles **3** 1 People take the seed pods from the cacao tree. 2 People leave the seed pods in the sun. 3 They throw away the outside and keep the seeds. 4 Machines grind and heat the seeds. 5 People put sugar and milk into the liquid. 6 They put the liquid in molds. **4** 1 rice 2 water 3 holes 4 pull **5** free answers

Page 34–35 **1** 1 Tiles go on walls and floors. 2 Pipes carry water. 3 Concrete can be a liquid. 4 Wires carry electricity. 5 Plaster goes on walls. **2** 1 electricity 2 wood 3 wall 4 garden 5 block 6 concrete **3** 1 false 2 true 3 true 4 false 5 false 6 true **4** free answers

Page 36–37 **1** 1 pages 2 cover 3 print 4 dots 5 glue **2** 1 Authors write the words. 2 Editors check the words. 3 Other people draw pictures or take photos. 4 Designers put the words and pictures into pages. 5 Machines print the pages. 6 Other machines cut the paper into pages. 7 People fix the pages together. **3** 1 author, editor, designer 2 computer, printing machine 3 pages, cover **4** 1 They use a computer. 2 They print 16 pages. 3 Thousands of very small dots. 4 They check the words. 5 They sewed them together.

Page 38–39 **1** 1 circuit board 2 screen 3 case 4 camera **2** 1 electricity 2 electronic 3 circuits 4 plastic 5 cameras **3** 1 true 2 false 3 false 4 false **4** 1 cell phone 2 circuit 3 screen 4 case 5 microchip 6 electronic 7 program 8 camera **5** free answers

Page 40–41 **1** 1 drawing 2 sensors 3 digital skeleton 4 digital characters **2** 1 Computer games are made with computer programs. 2 Digital skeletons are made of lines. 3 People play new computer games to check them. 4 Digital characters are people in computer games. 5 Sensors tell computers how a person moves. **3** 1 People draw the characters in the game. 2 They use computers to make digital skeletons. 3 People add faces, clothes, and colors to the skeleton. 4 They check the game. 5 People sell the game on the internet or in stores. **4** 1 computer 2 sensor 3 person 4 skeleton 5 program 6 digital

Page 42–43 **1** 1 landfill 2 river 3 electricity 4 recycling center 5 cans 6 sort **2** 1 recycle 2 recycling 3 use, recycled 4 products **3** 1 When we make products, we use energy. 2 Every day, people throw away millions of products. 3 Most waste goes to landfills. 4 Some waste goes in rivers. 5 We can recycle old products. **4** 1 There are 19 kilometers of wool in the Ferrari. 2 There are 35,000 parts in a car. 3 People make 48,000,000 cars every year. 4 Machines print 16 pages on one piece of paper. 5 To make one car, we make 28 metric tons of waste.

Subject Area

The World of Science & Technology

Topics & Curriculum Links

types of sound (Science; Music)
sound waves (Science)
how the human voice works (Science; Music)
musical instruments (Music)
rhythm (Music)
recording music (Technology; Music)
machines (Science)
countries (Geography)
quantities (Mathematics)
sizes and measurements (Mathematics)

Vocabulary

musical instruments; parts of the body; products; animals; transportation; machines; numbers; measurements; countries

Grammar

present simple; present continuous; past simple; question forms; imperative; adjectives; prepositions; adverbs

Teaching Ideas

See also pages 6–7 for general ideas that you can adapt. Or go to **www.oup.com/elt/teacher/readanddiscover**

Musical Instruments

After reading Chapter 4, students do research, using books or the Internet, to find more musical instruments in English. Then they present their findings in a big version of the chart on page 30 of the Reader.

A Sounds Poster

After completing Project 1, students make a class poster to present all the sounds that students have included in their posters.

READ & TALK A Music Survey

After completing Project 2, students collect the survey information from the class. They can do this by listening to each student giving their information in turn, or by collecting the information in a big version of the chart on page 45 of the Reader.

READ & TALK A Sounds Quiz

Bring in a number of objects that students know the names for in English. Put up a screen and behind the screen, drop an object onto a table. In small groups, students guess what the object is. Or bring in objects that make different noises and present each object's noise from behind the screen. Students can say or write what they think the objects are. Students can then organize their own sounds quiz on another day.

Activities Answers

Page 24–25 **1** 1 waves 2 shout 3 voice 4 push 5 molecule 6 sound waves **2** 1 shout 2 voice 3 molecules 4 move 5 waves 6 fast **3** 1 The girl is shouting 2 Her voice is pushing the molecules through the air. 3 Other people can hear her. 4 Sound moves at 350 meters per second. 5 The sound of a bus moves faster than the bus. 6 What sounds can you hear now? **4** free answers

Page 26–27 **1** 1 guitar 2 high 3 low 4 baby 5 truck **2** 1 false 2 true 3 true 4 false 5 false 6 false **3** 1 low 2 high 3 sound 4 string 5 guitar 6 thick 7 thin 8 vibrate 9 truck 10 frequency **4** 1 Things That Make a High Sound – a thin guitar string, a baby's cry, a bird's song Things That make a Low Sound – a truck, a plane, a thick guitar string

Page 28–29 **1** 1 air 2 mouth 3 throat 4 chest 5 vocal cords 6 lungs **2** 1 lower 2 higher 3 higher 4 lower 5 higher **3** 1 throat 2 speak 3 mouth 4 longer 5 high 6 notes **4** 1 They are in your throat. 2 They vibrate. 3 A woman's voice. 4 They can sing two notes at the same time.

Page 30–31 **1** 1 drum 2 flute 3 violin 4 cello 5 guitar 6 cymbals 7 clarinet 8 trumpet Wind Instruments – flute, clarinet, trumpet Percussion Instruments – drum, cymbals Stringed Instruments – violin, cello, guitar **2** 1 hits 2 percussion 3 stringed 4 bow 5 Trumpets 6 air **3** free answers **4** free answers

Page 32–33 **1** 1 gamelan 2 world 3 floor 4 orchestra 5 thumb **2** 1 false 2 true 3 true 4 false 5 false 6 true 7 false 8 false **3** 1 play 2 strings 3 streets 4 notes 5 orchestras 6 floor **4** 1 A sitar is a stringed instrument from India. 2 A bandoneon is a wind instrument from Argentina. 3 A gamelan is an orchestra from Indonesia. 4 A koto is a stringed instrument from Japan.

Page 34–35 **1** 1 conductor 2 musicians 3 instruments 4 flat 5 orchestra **2** 1 concert 2 musician 3 instrument 4 listen 5 watch 6 sound 7 bounce 8 wall 9 echo 10 panel **3** 1 musicians 2 conductor 3 help 4 practice 5 hall 6 walls **4** 1 He was one of the greatest musicians. 2 He was from Salzburg. 3 It's in Austria. 4 free answers

Page 36–37 **1** 1 true 2 false 3 true 4 false 5 true 6 false **2** 1 You tap your foot when you listen to music. 2 There are different types of rhythm in music. 3 The rhythm of a marching band is always the same. 4 The rhythm of flamenco music gets faster and slower. **3** 1 There are different types of rhythm. 2 The rhythm of a rock band is strong. 3 Flamenco music is from Spain. 4 Flamenco dancing is very exciting. **4** free answers

Page 38–39 **1** 1 MP3 player 2 digital signals 3 musicians 4 recording studio 5 microphone 6 sound engineer **2** 1 A songwriter writes a song. 2 Musicians practice the song. 3 The musicians go to a recording studio. 4 The musicians play the song in front of a microphone. 5 A sound engineer records the song. **3** 1 Today, people have MP3 ~~songs~~ players. 2 They ~~can't~~ can listen to their MP3 player in the streets. 3 A ~~microphone~~ songwriter writes songs. 4 A sound engineer works in a ~~store~~ recording studio. 5 A sound engineer ~~doesn't~~ does have a computer. **4** 1 They listen in the streets. 2 In a recording studio. 3 A sound engineer records the song. 4 free answers

Page 40–41 **1** 1 true 2 false 3 false 4 true 5 true 6 false **2** 1 About 100 years ago, people had record players. 2 Later, they listened to jukeboxes in cafes. 3 Today, people can buy music on the Internet. 4 Compact discs are called CDs. 5 Do you have an MP3 player? **3** 1 computer 2 Internet 3 records 4 music 5 song 6 jukebox 7 café 8 coins 9 play 10 listen **4** songs, player, everywhere, Internet, CDs, home

Page 42–43 **1** 1 street 2 cat 3 earphones 4 wind 5 car 6 jackhammer **2** 1 measure 2 jackhammer 3 bad 4 be 5 hear **3** 1 measure 2 bad 3 animals 4 car 5 coming 6 listen **4** 1 About 50 decibels. 2 No, it's a loud sound. 3 Yes it is. 4 free answers 5 free answers

3 Super Structures

Subject Area

The World of Science & Technology

Topics & Curriculum Links

materials and components (Science; Technology)
structures in the environment (Geography)
sizes and measurements (Mathematics)
shapes (Technology; Mathematics)
architecture (Art; Technology)
places and countries (Geography)
dates and events (History)
structures made by animals (Science)

Vocabulary

materials; structures; buildings; shapes; transportation; weather animals; measurements; numbers; months; places; countries; continents

Grammar

present simple; past simple; question forms; imperative; adjectives; prepositions; adverbs

Teaching Ideas

See also pages 5–7 for general ideas that you can adapt. Or go to **www.oup.com/elt/teacher/readanddiscover**

A Structures Graph

After completing Project 1, students make a graph to show the relative heights and silhouettes of the structures that they have chosen. They can use the model on page 8 of the Reader. They can write about the graph like this: *[Name of structure] is ... meters tall / long / wide ... [Name of structure] is the tallest / longest / widest ... [Name of structure] is taller / longer / wider than [Name of structure].*

READ & TALK A Design Competition

After completing Project 2, students present their design to the rest of the class. They can talk or write about their design like this: *My structure is called ... It's a / an ... It's made of ... It has ... It's for ...* They then display all the designs together, and students write comments on each other's design. Or they can vote for their favorite design.

READ & TALK Secret Structures

Choose a super structure from the Reader, then describe it to the class without saying its name. *It's ... tall / long. It's made of ... It has ... It's a ... in ... It's for ...* Or you can ask students to guess the structure by asking questions, for example *How tall / long is it? What's it made of? Where is it? What's it for?* Then ask students to do the same in pairs, taking turns to describe a structure from the Reader, or a structure in their country.

Activities Answers

Pages 24–25 **1** 1 Laerdal Tunnel 2 Seikan Tunnel 3 Laerdal Tunnel 4 Seikan Tunnel **2** 1 true 2 true 3 true 4 false 5 false **3** 1 under 2 concrete 3 Japan 4 Norway **4** 1 metal 2 longest 3 25 kilometers 4 under 5 through **5** 1 A 2 B 3 B 4 B 5 A 6 A

Pages 26–27 **1** 1 overground 2 longest 3 deck 4 suspension **2** 1 beam bridge 2 deck 3 pillar 4 suspension bridge 5 tower 6 cable 7 deck 8 anchorage **3** 1 bridge 2 water 3 beam 4 cable 5 deck 6 pillar 7 tower 8 anchorage **4** 1 The pillars carry the deck. 2 The cables and towers carry the deck. 3 They move a little when it's windy. 4 The Tacoma Bridge in the USA collapsed. 5 free answer

Pages 28–29 **1** 1 Burj Dubai 2 Taipei 101 3 Petronas Twin Towers 4 Sears Tower 5 Shanghai World Financial Center **2** 1 8mm 2 92 cm 3 900m 4 10mm 5 100cm 6 1,000m **3** 1 shorter 2 taller 3 tallest 4 taller 5 shorter **4** 1 It was built in Chicago. 2 It's 818 meters tall. 3 They are called the Petronas Twin Towers. 4 free answer

Pages 30–31 **1** 1 arch dam 2 reservoir 3 curve 4 gravity dam 5 reservoir 6 concrete **2** 1 false 2 true 3 false 4 true 5 true **3** 1 rain 2 Switzerland 3 heavy 4 concrete 5 curved 6 water **4** 1 It's a gravity dam. 2 It's in Switzerland. 3 The curve holds back the water. 4 The weight holds back the water. 5 free answer

Pages 32–33 **1** 1 National Stadium 2 Terminal 3 3 National Stadium 4 National Stadium 5 Terminal 3 **2** 1 China, planes 2 nest, metal, pipes **3** 1 color 2 Olympics 3 super 4 airport terminals 5 metal **4** 1 They were in 2008. 2 It's the capital of China. 3 It's red. 4 It's made of metal. 5 free answer

Pages 34–35 **1** 1 millennium 2 days 3 months 4 circle 5 wind 6 shape **2** 1 January 2 February 3 March 4 April 5 May 6 June 7 July 8 August 9 September 10 October 11 November 12 December **3** 1 materials, shapes 2 London, dome 3 skyscraper, day **4** 1 The O2 is a dome. 2 There are 12 months in a year. 3 Every floor can rotate a full circle. 4 There are 365 days in a year. 5 The rotating skyscraper uses energy from the wind.

Pages 36–37 **1** 1 bricks 2 concrete 3 ice 4 glass 5 mud 6 metal 7 plastic 8 wood **2** 1 true 2 false 3 false 4 false 5 true 6 false **3** 1 Biosphere 2; 2 Ice Hotel 3 Ice Hotel 4 Biosphere 2; 5 Biosphere 2; 6 free answer **4** 1 Ice Hotel is made of ice. 2 Every year Ice Hotel is built again. 3 It is open from December to April. 4 The drinking glasses are made of ice. 5 Biosphere 2 is made of glass and metal. 6 There is a rainforest in Biosphere 2.

Pages 38–39 **1** 1 Halley 6; 2 Poseidon Undersea Resort 3 Halley 6; 4 Halley 6 **2** Poseidon Undersea Resort: water, submarine, fish, hotel, ocean; Halley 6: cold, skis, wind, ice, research **3** 1 under 2 plastic 3 on 4 moves 5 weather **4** 1 It's in Fiji. 2 It's in the Antarctic. 3 You travel by submarine. 4 It can be less than -50 degrees centigrade. 5 free answer

Pages 40–41 **1** 1 astronaut 2 earth 3 research 4 rocket 5 shuttle 6 space **2** 1 350; 2 16; 3 27,700; 4 8; 5 1998; **3** 1 astronaut 2 ISS 3 Earth **4** 1 It's about 350 kilometers above Earth. 2 It's a research station. 3 It went into space in 1998. 4 No astronauts went with it. 5 They do spacewalks outside the ISS. 6 Yes, you can.

Pages 42–43 **1** 1 false 2 true 3 true 4 false 5 true 6 free answer **2** 1 Animals can build super structures too. 2 Termite mounds are termite skyscrapers. 3 Wombats dig about 2 meters per hour. 4 Termites build their homes with mud. 5 Beaver dams can be a kilometer long. **3** 1 super structures 2 skyscrapers 3 curve 4 underground 5 bridge 6 concrete 7 tunnels 8 road 9 metal 10 dam 11 over 12 long 13 glass

3 Your Five Senses

Subject Area

The World of Science & Technology

Topics & Curriculum Links

human body and senses (Science)
light and sound (Science; Music)
daily life (Civics)
disabilities (Science; Civics)
keeping safe (Civics)
machines (Technology)
animals (Science)
food (Science)
quantities and measurements (Mathematics)

Vocabulary

senses; human body; daily activities; hobbies; musical instruments; food; animals; numbers; places; weather

Grammar

present simple; present continuous; question forms; imperative; adjectives; prepositions; adverbs

Teaching Ideas

See also pages 6–7 for general ideas that you can adapt. Or go to **www.oup.com/elt/teacher/readanddiscover**

READ & TALK A Senses Presentation

After completing Project 1, students present their chosen sense to the rest of the class. They can talk or write about it like this: *This sense is sight / hearing / smell / taste / touch. I see / hear / smell / taste / touch things with my ... With this sense I can ...* Students then display all the designs together, and vote for the most important sense. They can then create a five-bar chart to present the results of the vote.

READ & TALK A Senses Test

Bring in a number of things that students can hear, smell, taste, or touch. Individual students or groups then take turns to be blindfolded and to try to guess what the things are. Any students who want to participate will have to wait in an area of the classroom where they can't see the answers! Students can say or write what they think the things are. Students can then organize their own test on another day.

Sense Detectives

In small groups or as individuals, students write a list of things that a sense lets us do, for example, things that we can see, hear, touch, smell, or taste. They then share their ideas with the class, and collect all the ideas on the board. They can then do the same with other senses. To make this more challenging, students can do this with one letter, for example, list the things that you can see that start with the letter 'm', or they can list something for each letter of the alphabet.

Activities Answers

Pages 24–25 **1** 1 photo 2 eye 3 lamp 4 sun 5 traffic lights 6 rainbow **2** 1 watch 2 read 3 see 4 watch 5 look **3** 1 see 2 detect 3 three 4 white 5 dark 6 reflect 7 colors 8 lamp **4** 1 colors 2 eyes 3 lamp 4 photos 5 rainbow 6 dark 7 prism

Pages 26–27 **1** 1 iris 2 eyelid 3 pupil 4 eyelashes 5 sclera **2** 1 false 2 false 3 true 4 true 5 true **3** 1 pupil 2 lens 3 retina 4 optic cells 5 optic nerve **4** 1 The retina is at the back of the eye. 2 Your pupils open more in the dark to let more light in. 3 The retina has millions of optic cells. 4 free answer

Pages 28–29 **1** 1 I can listen to my favorite music. 2 I can hear sounds from the right or the left. 3 I can listen to people when they talk to me. 4 I can hear when the telephone rings. **2** 1 flute 2 bass drum 3 tuba 4 whistle 5 wind chimes 6 jet plane 7 motorcycle 8 clock **3** 1 high 2 loud 3 low 4 soft 5 high 6 loud **4** 1 high 2 tuba 3 loud 4 sound 5 hear 6 motorcycle 7 flute 8 soft 9 music 10 listen **5** free answers

Pages 30–31 **1** 1 vibrations 2 ear canal 3 eardrum 4 ossicles 5 cochlea 6 auditory nerve **2** 1 Sound vibrations go into the ear canal. 2 The eardrum vibrates. 3 Then the ossicles vibrate too. 4 The cochlea detects the vibrations. 5 The auditory nerve collects the information. 6 The information goes to the brain. **3** 1 true 2 false 3 false 4 false 5 false **4** bones, ossicles, vibration, eardrum, ear canal, cochlea, auditory nerve, hearing aid, implants, microphone

Pages 32–33 **1** 1 perfume 2 bad eggs 3 pizza 4 flowers 5 food waste 6 cookies **2** 1 They smell good: cookies, pizza, perfume, flowers; They smell bad: food waste, bad eggs; They're good to eat: pizza, cookies **3** 1 It doesn't smell very good. 2 I think it's a skunk! 3 Yes, I think there's a fire! 4 Are you making cookies? 5 They're probably bad. **4** 1 How does food waste smell? It smells terrible. 2 Do you like the smell of pizza? free answer 3 Do poisonous chemicals smell good? No, they don't. 4 What is your favorite smell? free answer

Pages 34–35 **1** 1 particles 2 nostrils 3 nasal passages 4 olfactory cells 5 olfactory nerve **2** 1 clouds, air 2 nostrils, nose 3 particles, nasal 4 olfactory, different 5 nerve, brain **3** 1 They open wider when something smells good. 2 They are in your nasal passages. 3 You have about 5 million olfactory cells. 4 It recognizes familiar smells. **4** 1 cell 2 nerve 3 clouds 4 nostril 5 passages 6 olfactory; the secret word is: particles

Pages 36–37 **1** 1 lemon juice 2 salt 3 orange peel 4 French fries 5 sugar 6 honey **2** 1 Salty 2 sweet 3 salt 4 bitter 5 sour 6 sugar **3** 1 Many people add salt to make foods salty. 2 We can add sugar to make foods sweet. 3 Your tongue detects the tastes of your food. 4 Ice cream usually has a lot of sugar in it. 5 Meat and cheese have a savory taste. 6 We can make marmalade from bitter orange peel. **4 & 5** free answers

Pages 38–39 **1** 1 tongue 2 bumps 3 tastes 4 nerves 5 brain **2** 1 false 2 true 3 false 4 true 5 false 6 true **3** 1 tastes 2 food 3 bumps 4 surface 5 tongue 6 sides 7 taste buds 8 front 9 nerves 10 back. **4** 1 There are about 10,000 taste buds on your tongue. 2 Most of them are at the front, back, and sides of your tongue. 3 Because they get old quickly. 4 It only takes about two weeks. 5 Because your senses of taste and smell work together.

Pages 40–41 **1** 1 It feels soft. 2 It feels smooth. 3 It feels hot. 4 It feels hard. 5 It feels cold. 6 It feels rough. **2** 1 fire 2 glass 3 feathers **3** 1 hard 2 cold 3 rough 4 hot 5 smooth 6 soft **4** 1 soft 2 rough 3 hot 4 cool 5 smooth 6 hard 7 temperature 8 texture 9 warm 10 cold

Pages 42–43 **1** 1 face 2 neck 3 hands 4 feet **2** 1 My skin has millions of nerve endings. 2 Nerve endings detect temperature and textures. 3 My face and neck are very sensitive. 4 I can't feel my skin when it's very cold. 5 Pain tells my brain that I'm in danger. **3** 1 touch, safe 2 endings, skin 3 signals, danger 4 nose, numb 5 feel, hurt **4** 1 tongue 2 eyes 3 sounds 4 nostrils 5 bitter 6 retina 7 textures 8 cochlea 9 smooth 10 perfume

3 Amazing Minibeasts

Subject Area
The Natural World

Topics & Curriculum Links
classification (Science)
life cycles (Science)
minibeasts in the environment (Science; Geography)
senses (Science)
parts of the body (Science)
plants and pollination (Science)
quantities and measurements (Mathematics)

Vocabulary
minibeasts; other animals; parts of the body; senses; food; plants; numbers; places

Grammar
present simple; question forms; imperative; adjectives; prepositions

Teaching Ideas

See also pages 6–7 for general ideas that you can adapt. Or go to **www.oup.com/elt/teacher/readanddiscover**

READ & TALK Minibeast Life Cycles

After reading Chapter 5, students do research, using books or the Internet, about a minibeast life cycle. They can present their findings in the form of a life cycle diagram, similar to the model on page 13 of the Reader. They can talk or write about the life cycle using the language model on page 33 of the Reader, for example: *The ... lays an egg. A ... comes out of the egg. The ... becomes a ... Then the ... becomes a ...*

READ & TALK A Minibeasts Survey

After completing Project 1, students collect all the minibeast information from the class. They can do this by listening to each student giving their information in turn, or by collecting the class information in a big chart on the board. They then calculate the total number of different minibeasts seen. Finally they make a bar chart showing the number of different types of minibeast seen during the week.

READ & TALK Minibeast Factfiles

After completing Project 2, students choose a minibeast, and do research using books or the Internet. Then they write about their findings and display the information with pictures. They can write about it like this: *It's a / an ... It has ... It's ... It can ... It lives ... It eats ...* Students can then present their animal to the class. Or students can talk about their animal without saying its name, and ask the class to guess the animal.

READ & TALK Mystery Minibeasts

Students choose one of the minibeasts from the Reader. Then students ask the class to guess their mystery minibeast by asking questions like the ones on page 24 of the Reader, for example: *Does it have ... legs? Does its body have sections? Can it ...? Is it [color]?* The student with the mystery minibeast can only answer *yes* or *no* to the questions.

Activities Answers

Pages 24–25 **1** Insects: grasshopper, fly, bee, ant, beetle; Arachnids: spider, scorpion; Myriapods: millipede, centipede; Annelids: leech, earthworm; Molluscs: snail, slug; **2** 1 bee (3) 2 scorpion (4) 3 snail (2) 4 earthworm (1) **3** free answers

Pages 26–27 **1** 1 head 2 wing 3 leg 4 thorax 5 abdomen **2** bones, cover, grow, small, new **3** 1 can 2 don't want 3 Some 4 isn't 5 sometimes 6 can't **4** 1 They are black, white, and red. 2 Most insects have three parts. 3 They are called the head, thorax, and abdomen. 4 It comes off. 5 They use their bodies for camouflage.

Pages 28–29 **1** 1 false 2 true 3 false 4 true 5 true 6 false **2** 1 These are antennae. 2 These eyes can see light and dark. 3 These eyes can see things move. **3** 1 Insects 2 Insects 3 People 4 Insects 5 Insects 6 People and insects **4** free answers

Pages 30–31 **1** moths, ants, bees, grasshoppers, fireflies **2** female, male, female, male, female **3** 1 touch 2 dance 3 smell 4 sound 5 light 6 sing **4** 1 Moths 2 Fireflies 3 Bees 4 Grasshoppers 5 Ants **5** 1 They move their legs up and down to make a singing sound. 2 They make light with their abdomen. 3 They dance to tell other bees where there is food.

Pages 32–33 **1** 1 earthworm 2 scorpion 3 plants 4 soil 5 butterfly 6 egg 7 ant 8 slug 9 beetle; the secret word is: minibeast **2** 1 lay eggs ✓, have live babies ✗ 2 in soil ✓, on plants ✗ 3 on plants ✓, in soil ✗ 4 have live babies ✓, lay eggs ✗ **3** Diagram: egg, pupa; Text: butterfly, eggs, caterpillar, caterpillar, pupa, butterfly, pupa, insect, wings

Pages 34–35 **1** 1 The leafcutter ants find leaves. 2 They carry the leaves to their nest. 3 Fungus grows. 4 They eat the fungus. **2** 1 false 2 false 3 true 4 true 5 true **3** Leafcutter ants: They carry leaves. They find leaves. They eat fungus. Honeybees: They live in a hive. They make honey. They keep honey in honeycombs. Leafcutter ants and honeybees: They are insects. They work together in groups.

Pages 36–37 **1** 1 dragonfly 2 wasp 3 earthworm 4 snail 5 ant **2** 1 ant 2 dragonfly 3 snail 4 wasp **3** 1 nests 2 paper 3 saliva 4 queen 5 larvae **4** 1 Earthworms and ants live underground. 2 They lay their eggs on leaves in the water. 3 They live in a nest.

Pages 38–39 **1** 1 liquid 2 poison 3 spider 4 leaves 5 web 6 mice **2** 1 All spiders can make silk: true 2 All spiders make webs: false 3 All spiders hunt: false 4 The wolf spider makes a web: false 5 The wolf spider eats mice: true **3** Spiders: two; eight; six or eight; liquid food from insects, mice, and frogs; silk and webs; Insects: three; six; some have two eyes and some also have extra eyes; leaves, fungus, nectar, honey; hives and nests **4** free answers

Pages 40–41 **1** 1 mosquito 2 ant 3 beetle 4 moth 5 locust **2** 1 again and again 2 Some 3 can 4 Mosquitoes 5 Female 6 food crops **3** mosquito **4** free answers

Pages 42–43 **1** 1 frog 2 bat 3 fish 4 silkworm 5 earthworm 6 bee **2** 1 Fish, frogs, and bats eat minibeasts. 2 Silkworms give us silk. 3 Earthworms let air and water into soil. 4 Bees give us honey. 5 Insects move pollen from flower to flower. **3 example answers** Problems: They can sting. Some minibeasts can bite. Sometimes the bite is poisonous and can make people sick. Locusts make problems for farmers, because they eat a lot of food crops. Some moths eat clothes and some beetles eat wood. Good things: Bees give us honey. Silkworms give us silk to make silk fabric. Earthworms let air and water in when they move through the soil. Insects move pollen from flower to flower. This is called pollination. **4** 1 butterfly 2 fireflies 3 snail 4 wasp 5 leafcutter ant 6 dragonfly 7 scorpion 8 millipede 9 spider 10 mosquito

Animals in the Air

Subject Area
The Natural World

Topics & Curriculum Links
animals (Science)
animal classification (Science)
parts of the body (Science)
how animals move (Science)
animal homes (Science)
food (Science)
weather and climate (Science)
sizes and measurements (Mathematics)
quantities (Mathematics)
places and countries (Geography)
dates and events (History)

Vocabulary
animals; parts of the body; animal movements; plants; places; numbers; measurements; countries; continents

Grammar
present simple; present continuous; past simple; question forms; imperative; adjectives; prepositions; adverbs

Teaching Ideas

See also pages 6–7 for general ideas that you can adapt. Or go to **www.oup.com/elt/teacher/readanddiscover**

READ & TALK An Animal Presentation
After completing Project 2, students present their animal to the rest of the class. They can write or talk about their animal like this: *This animal is a ... It's a bird / an insect / a mammal. It flies / jumps / glides in the air. Its body has / is ... This animal is special because it can ...* Or students can talk about their animal without saying its name, and ask the class to guess the animal.

READ & TALK Which Animal Is It?
Choose a photo of one of the animals from the Reader and without saying the animal's name, describe the photo and ask students to guess which animal it is. Describe what the animal looks like, and what it's doing. Students can then do this in small groups or pairs.

An Animals in the Air Survey
Ask students to spend 30 minutes watching from their window at home, and to write down the names of all the animals in the air that they see. Students can then find the words for the animals in English and report back to the class.

Activities Answers

Page 24–25 **1** 1 Animals that fly can move around fast. 2 Flying helps some animals to stay safe. 3 Some flying birds live in high places. 4 Some birds fly to hunt other animals **2** 1 find 2 collect 3 make 4 escape 5 hunt **3** 1 false 2 true 3 true 4 false 5 false 6 true **4** 1 It helps them to stay safe. 2 They find nectar in flowers. 3 Owls hunt mice. 4 Many birds make their homes in tall trees. 5 A stork's nest can be 2 meters across. 6 Storks make their nests in high places.

Page 26–27 **1** 1 feather 2 tail 3 bone 4 wing 5 air spaces 6 wingspan **2** 1 feathers 2 warm 3 light 4 big 5 was **3** 1 Flight feathers help birds to fly. 2 An Andean condor can have a 3-meter wingspan. 3 A hummingbird can have a 6-centimeter wingspan. 4 A Giant Teratorn had a wingspan of up to 7 meters. 5 The Giant Teratorn lived about 6 million years ago. **4** 1 feathers 2 body 3 light 4 bones 5 dry 6 tail 7 wing 8 wingspan

Page 28–29 **1** 1 swift 2 peregrine falcon 3 bar-tailed godwit 4 swallow **2** 1 It's the bar-tailed godwit. 2 It's the swift. 3 It's the swallow. 4 It's the peregrine falcon. **3** 1 watch 2 stop 3 need 4 sleep 5 turn 6 spend 7 rest 8 dive **4** 1 16,500 2 more than 200 kilometers per hour 3 swallows 4 swifts

Page 30–31 **1** 1 The sun makes the land warm. 2 The land makes the air warm. 3 Warm air currents go up. 4 Birds go up on the air currents. 5 The birds soar high in the air. **2** 1 sun 2 mountains 3 currents **3** 1 Bar-headed geese can't fly over mountains. false 2 Some vultures fly higher than planes. true 3 Eagles can soar on warm air currents. true 4 Condors don't have very wide wings. false 5 The Himalayas are very high mountains. true **4** 1 Ruppell's vultures 2 When it's sunny. 3 Long and wide. 4 Bar-headed geese.

Page 32–33 **1** 1 fly 2 bee 3 moth 4 dragonfly 5 butterfly 6 mosquito **2** 1 four 2 two 3 four 4 four 5 two **3** 1 300 2 50 3 350 4 30 5 70 **4** 1 bees 2 wings 3 thorax 4 insects 5 mosquito 6 kilometer The secret word is Meganeura

Page 34–35 **1** Birds – duck, starling Hunting Birds – eagle, falcon Insects – bee, locust, moth **2** 1 fly 2 hunting 3 insect 4 farmers 5 swarms **3** 1 group 2 join 3 dark 4 swarm 5 plants 6 hungry 7 farmer 8 flock **4** 1 When they move to a new place. 2 dark clouds 3 When they are moving to a new home. 4 All the green plants that they find.

Page 36–37 **1** 1 webs 2 flea 3 springtail 4 insect 5 leg 6 spider 7 minibeast 8 grasshopper **2** 1 true 2 false 3 false 4 true 5 false **3** 1 back legs 2 other animals 3 catch insects 4 on insects 5 into the air 6 body length **4** 1 20 times its body length 2 insects 3 by jumping 4 their tails

Page 38–39 **1** 1 wing 2 membrane 3 leg 4 sound 5 echo 6 insect **2** 1 true 2 false 3 true 4 false 5 true **3** 1 Bats usually rest in the day. 2 Bats make sounds that bounce off things. 3 Bats use echolocation to find their way at night. 4 Bats have wings with long, thin bones. 5 Bats are the only mammals that can fly. **4** 1 flying foxes 2 echolocation 3 a membrane of skin 4 fruit, flowers and pollen

Page 40–41 **1** 1 gibbon 2 springbok gazelle 3 flying squirrel 4 kangaroo **2** 1 jump 2 travel 3 swing 4 glide 5 pronk **3** 1 3 meters 2 jumping and swinging between trees 3 more than 30 kilometers per hour 4 membranes **4** 1 kite 2 mammal 3 high 4 fence 5 branch 6 straight 7 membrane 8 fast 9 far 10 body

Page 42–43 **1** 1 Gliding leaf frogs have membranes between their fingers and toes. They use these membranes to glide on the air. 2 Paradise tree snakes can glide about 100 meters through the air. 3 Flying fish have big fins that look like wings. They can glide in the air for hundreds of meters. **2** 1 membranes 2 meters 3 body 4 reptiles **3** 1 swift 2 stork 3 eagle 4 dragonfly 5 flying fox 6 starling 7 flea 8 hummingbird 9 swallow 10 gibbon **4** free answers

3 Life in Rainforests

Subject Area

The Natural World

Topics & Curriculum Links

tropical rainforests and the environment (Science; Civics)
tropical rainforests around the world (Geography)
animal habitats (Science)
plants (Science)
weather (Science)
food (Science)
rivers (Geography; Civics)
rainforest people (Geography; Civics)
materials and products (Science)
continents and countries (Geography)
sizes and measurements (Mathematics)

Vocabulary

plants; animals; weather; food; materials; parts of the body; transportation; measurements; numbers; places; countries; continents

Grammar

present simple; present continuous; question forms; imperative; adjectives; prepositions; adverbs

Teaching Ideas

See also pages 6–7 for general ideas that you can adapt. Or go to **www.oup.com/elt/teacher/readanddiscover**

Rainforest Layers Research

After reading Chapter 2, students do research, using books or the Internet, about which animals live in which rainforest layers, for a chosen tropical rainforest. Students can then make a class poster showing the different animals in the different layers. They can also add short texts about the animals.

READ & TALK Which Rainforest Is It?

After completing activity 4 on page 43 of the Reader, students write a quiz with new questions, but using similar structures, for example: *It has ...; ... is here; ... live here.* Students then read out their questions for others to guess which rainforest it is.

READ & TALK Mystery Animals

Students choose one of the animals from the Reader. Then students ask the class to guess their mystery animal by asking questions, for example: *Is it big / small? Is it [color]? Does it have ...? Can it ...? Does it live ...?* The student with the mystery animals can only answer *yes* or *no* to the questions.

Activities Answers

Page 24–25 **1** 1 North America 2 Central America 3 South America 4 Africa 5 Europe 6 Asia 7 Australasia 8 Equator 9 The Tropics 10 Amazon rainforest 11 Congo rainforest 12 Madagascar 13 India 14 Australia **2** free answers **3** 1 6% 2 50% 3 750, 1,500, 400, 150 **4** 1 All the tropical rainforests are near the equator. 2 Most of them are in the Tropics. 3 The Amazon rainforest in South America 4 The Congo rainforest in Africa 5 Central America, Madagascar, India, Australia, and on the islands near Australia.

Page 26–27 **1** 1 emergent layer 2 canopy 3 understory 4 forest floor **2** 1 understory 2 emergent layer 3 canopy 4 forest floor 5 forest floor 6 emergent layer 7 understory 8 canopy **3** 1 Emergent layer: eagles, bats; Canopy: monkeys, toucans; Understory: jaguars, tree frogs; Forest floor: anteaters, insects **4** 1 Eagles and bats live in the emergent layer. 2 Monkeys and toucans live in the canopy. 3 Jaguars and tree frogs live in the understory. 4 Anteaters and insects live on the forest floor.

Page 28–29 **1** 1 plant 2 leaves 3 branches 4 nest 5 tree hole **2** 1 true 2 true 3 true 4 false 5 false 6 false **3** 1 bananas 2 wood 3 latex 4 nuts 5 clothes, bags **4** 1 are 2 grow 3 can 4 use 5 gives 6 make 7 get 8 sleep

Page 30–31 **1** 1 piranha 2 anaconda 3 congo 4 mekong 5 amazon **2** 1 The Mekong River is: ✗ bigger than the Amazon, ✓ in Asia 2 The Amazon isn't: ✓ a small river, ✗ the biggest rainforest river 3 The Amazon has more than 3,000: ✓ types of fish, ✗ smaller rivers. 4 An anaconda is: ✓ a snake, ✗ a fish 5 Rivers give people: ✗ food and light, ✓ food and water 6 Many rainforest people travel by: ✗ train, ✓ boat **3** 1 Many animals live in rainforest rivers. 2 Rivers give people water. 3 Rivers give people fish to eat. 4 Rivers are important for travel. 5 People travel by boat on rivers. 6 There aren't many roads in the Amazon. **4** **Example answers** 1 The River Amazon is in South America. It's the <u>biggest rainforest river</u>. It's about <u>6,400 kilometers long</u>. It has <u>more than 3,000 types of fish</u>. <u>Many animals</u> live in the River Amazon. People need the river because <u>it gives them fish to eat, and water</u>.

Page 32–33 **1** 1 fish 2 sloth 3 shellfish 4 platypus 5 worm 6 insects 7 chimpanzee 8 tiger **2** 1 sloths 2 tigers 3 platypuses 4 Chimpanzees **3** 1 Chimpanzees, Food: leaves, fruit, insects, other small animals. Sloths, Rainforest: Central and South American rainforest; Food leaves and fruit. Tigers, Rainforest: Asian rainforest. Platypuses, Rainforest: Australian rainforest; Food: insects, shellfish, worms **4** free answers

Page 34–35 **1** 1 butterfly 2 mantis 3 beetle 4 spider 5 rhino **2** The female Queen Alexandra's Birdwing is the biggest butterfly. Rhinoceros beetles have horns like rhinos. Tarantulas are probably the biggest spiders. Mantises can look like flowers. **3** 1 The Queen Alexandra's Birdwing lives in ~~India~~ <u>Papua New Guinea</u>. 2 Most of the minibeasts in rainforests are ~~spiders~~ <u>insects</u>. 3 Mantises ~~can't~~ <u>can</u> use camouflage. 4 Rhinoceros beetles have a ~~stinger~~ <u>horn</u> on their head. 5 Tarantulas live in ~~African~~ <u>South American</u> rainforests. 6 Tarantulas have ~~six~~ <u>eight</u> eyes.

Page 36–37 **1** 1 head 2 eye 3 wing 4 tail 5 feet **2** 1 colorful 2 babies 3 wings 4 58 5 can't 6 fast **3** 1 Australian King Parrot: It has a yellow circle around each eye. It's red, blue, green, and yellow; Hoatzin: Its babies can climb. It lives in the Amazon; Female Northern Cassowary: It has very big feet. It can be 2 meters tall; Hummingbird: It flaps its wings very fast. It's very small. **4** free answers

Page 38–39 **1** 1 flour 2 blowpipe 3 palm tree 4 deer 5 birds 6 hut; secret word: forest **2** 1 deer, birds 2 hut 3 flour 4 palm tree 5 blowpipe **3** 1 Sarawak, in Borneo, in Asia 2 two 3 sago flour, deer, smaller mammals, birds 4 Because other people cut down the trees. **4** free answers

Page 40–41 **1** 1 wood 2 furniture 3 sugar 4 coffee 5 flour 6 door 7 cow **2** 1 People cut down rainforest trees. 2 They get wood from the trees. 3 They sell the wood. 4 Other people make furniture, doors, and floors. **3** 1 Some farmers cut down rainforest trees. 2 They keep cows on the land. 3 Some farmers grow coffee or sugar. 4 They then sell the cows, coffee, and sugar. **4** 1 soil 2 slowly 3 die 4 homes 5 food 6 live

Page 42–43 **1** 1 Cut down rainforest trees. ✗ 2 Buy furniture made from rainforest wood. ✗ 3 Teach people about rainforests. ✓ 4 Buy recycled paper. ✓ 5 Buy coffee from farmers who cut down rainforest trees. ✗ **2** 1 people 2 plants 3 rivers 4 mammals 5 birds 6 minibeasts **3** 1 Sumatra 2 Indonesia 3 tigers 4 rainforests **4** 1 Amazon 2 Congo 3 Amazon 4 Asian 5 Australian 6 Asian 7 African 8 South American 9 Amazon 10 Asian

3 Wonderful Water

Subject Area

The Natural World

Topics & Curriculum Links

water and the environment (Science; Civics)
forms of water (Science)
water around the world (Geography)
floods and droughts; saving water (Science; Civics)
plants and animals (Science)
human body (Science)
life at home; sports (Civics)
sizes and percentages (Mathematics)

Vocabulary

sources of water; forms of water; seas and oceans; water cycle; weather; washing at home; animals; human body; transportation; sports; floods and rescue; measurements; numbers; places; countries; continents

Grammar

present simple; question forms; imperative; adjectives; prepositions

Teaching Ideas

See also pages 6–7 for general ideas that you can adapt.
Or go to **www.oup.com/elt/teacher/readanddiscover**

READ & TALK A Water Diary Survey

After completing Project 1, students collect all the diary information from the class. They can do this by listening to each student giving their information in turn, or by collecting the class information in a big chart on the board.

They then calculate the total amount of water they use for each activity, using these figures: glass of water: 0.25 liters; flushing the toilet: 9 liters; taking a shower: 27 liters; taking a bath: 80 liters; brushing teeth: 1 liter.

Then they make a five-bar chart showing how much water they use for all the activities. They can talk or write about the chart like this: *In our class, we use ... liters of water for drinking / flushing the toilet / taking showers / taking baths / brushing our teeth. We use the most / least water for ...*

Water Around the World

After completing Project 2, students do research, using books or the Internet, about water in another country, or for example, about rivers, lakes, or oceans around the world. They display their findings on a poster with pictures, maps, charts, etc. Students can work in groups, and posters can then be displayed together.

READ & TALK Animal Fact Files

Students choose a freshwater or saltwater animal, and do research using books or the Internet. Then they write about it and display the information with pictures. They can use the models in Chapters 7 and 8, for example: *It's a / an ... It has ... It lives ... It eats ...* Students can then present their animal to the class. Or students can talk about their animal without saying its name, and then ask the class to guess the animal.

Activities Answers

Pages 24–25 **1** 1 Ocean 2 Ocean 3 Sea 4 Ocean 5 Sea 6 Ocean 7 Ocean 8 Sea **2** 1 5; 2 30; 3 3; 4 70; 5 156; 6 15; 7 11,000 **3** 1 Atlantic Ocean 2 Arctic Ocean 3 Europe 4 North America 5 Pacific Ocean 6 Southern Ocean 7 Antarctica 8 South America 9 Australasia 10 Indian Ocean 11 Africa 12 Asia **4** free answer

Pages 26–27 **1** 1 false 2 false 3 true 4 false 5 true 6 false **2** 1 glacier 2 rain 3 soil 4 lake 5 cloud 6 cave 7 river **3** 1 is in glaciers 2 in rivers 3 is in reservoirs 4 water is in clouds 5 the water is in the soil 6 of the water is in caves

Pages 28–29 **1** 1 precipitation 2 stream 3 evaporation 4 river 5 ocean 6 sun **2** 7, 4, 1, 6, 2, 5, 3 **3** 1 reservoir; 2 dirty water; 3 clean water; 4 pipe; 5 home **4** 1 true 2 true 3 false 4 false

Pages 30–31 **1** 1 ✓ 2 ✓ 3 ✓ 4 ✗ 5 ✗ 6 ✓ 7 ✗ 8 ✗ 9 ✓ 10 ✓ **2** 1 the toilet 2 shower 3 I brush my teeth 4 dressed 5 my hair 6 I drink some water 7 I read a comic book 8 television 9 I cook 10 I wash the dishes **3** 1 27; 2 80; 3 9 **4** free answers

Pages 32–33 **1** 1 vegetables 2 fruit 3 boat 4 ship 5 animals 6 meat **2** 1 drink water 2 water to grow 3 by boat and by ship 4 is electricity made from water **3** 1 waterskiing 2 horse riding 3 diving 4 swimming 5 tennis 6 sailing 7 soccer 8 surfing; Water Sports: waterskiing, diving, swimming, sailing, surfing; Other Sports: horse riding, tennis, soccer

Pages 34–35 **1** 1 blood 2 kidneys 3 bones 4 brain 5 lungs **2** 1 brain 2 blood 3 bones 4 brain **3** 1 70; 2 4; 3 3; 4 8 **4** 1 About 70%. 2 Oxygen and food. 3 Three days. 4 We get dehydrated.

Pages 36–37 **1** 1 true 2 true 3 false 4 true 5 false 6 false **2** biggest meters big; elephants ocean animals oceans **3** 1 food (or fish) 2 oxygen 3 support **4** free answers

Pages 38–39 **1 & 2** Freshwater Animals: duck, frog, crocodile, beaver, hippo; Saltwater Animals: jellyfish, whale, shark **3** 1 eat other animals under water. 2 are land animals. 3 need water to keep their skin healthy. **4** free answers

Pages 40–41 **1** 1 too much rain 2 leave 3 boats and helicopters 4 Don't play **2** 1 roof 2 helicopter 3 house 4 boat 5 road 6 cars; The secret word is: floods **3** 1 road 2 helicopter 3 roof 4 house 5 boat 6 cars 7 police 8 firefighter 9 flood 10 river

Pages 42–43 **1** Don't turn off water. ✗ Turn off water. ✓ Take a shower. ✓ Take a bath. ✗ Collect rainwater. ✓ Don't collect rainwater. ✗ Don't throw things into rivers. ✓ Throw things into river. ✓ **2** free answers

3 Festivals Around the World

Subject Area

The World of Arts & Social Studies

Topics & Curriculum Links

dates and events (History)
life at home (Civics)
traditional celebrations (Civics)
places and countries (Geography)
food (Science)
clothes and costumes (Civics)
seasons, weather, and climate (Geography)
quantities (Mathematics)

Vocabulary

months, seasons; family; clothes; weather; food; plants; animals; parts of the body; numbers; places; countries; continents

Grammar

present simple; past simple; question forms; imperative; adjectives, prepositions; adverbs

Teaching Ideas

See also pages 6–7 for general ideas that you can adapt. Or go to **www.oup.com/elt/teacher/readanddiscover**

Festivals Around the World

After completing Project 1, students do more research, using books or the Internet, to find more festivals around the world for each month. Then they can make a class poster to present their findings.

READ & TALK A Festival Presentation

After completing Project 2, students make a poster about their chosen festival, adding pictures to illustrate the words that they have chosen. Then they present their festival to the rest of the class. They can write or talk about how they celebrate their festival like this: *[Festival] ... is in / on [month / date. We eat ... We wear ... We [activities]. The weather is usually ...*

READ & TALK Which Festival Is It?

Choose one of the festivals from the Reader, and without saying its name, read out one fact about it and asks students to guess which festival it is. Read out more facts, one at a time, until students guess the correct festival. You can use a point scoring system, for example, five points after one fact, three points after two facts, etc. Students can then do this in small groups or pairs.

Activities Answers

Page 24–25 **1** 1 parade 2 float 3 dress 4 costumes 5 cloak 6 street **2** 1 false 2 false 3 true 4 true 5 false 6 true **3** 1 big 2 people 3 people 4 winter 5 cloaks 6 fun **4** 1 Where is Rio de Janeiro? It's in Brazil. 2 When is the carnival in Rio de Janeiro? It's in February or March. 3 Is there music at the Rio de Janeiro festival? Yes, there is. 4 Where is Venice? It's in Italy. 5 Is the carnival in Venice in summer? No, it's in winter. 6 How is the weather at the Venice carnival? It's colder than in Brazil. **5** 1 free answers

Page 26–27 **1** 1 Diwali is sometimes in October. 2 At Diwali, people put lamps in their homes. 3 At Diwali, people think about their family and other people. 4 Hanukkah is usually in December. 5 Hanukkah is a Jewish festival. 6 At Hanukkah, people eat pancakes. **2** 1 festival 2 November 3 big 4 candles 5 presents 6 donuts **3** Festivals: carnival, Diwali, Hanukkah; Countries: Brazil, Italy, India; Months: February, October, December **4** 1 They put lamps in their homes. 2 It's in October or November. 3 They eat pancakes and donuts. 4 It's usually in December. **5** free answers

Page 28–29 **1** 1 Muslim 2 presents 3 toys 4 money 5 clothes 6 festival **2** 1 ✓ 2 ✗ 3 ✓ 4 ✗ 5 ✗ 6 ✓ 7 ✓ **3** 1 Eid is a big festival. 2 People give presents to their friends. 3 They think about other people. 4 People eat dates at Eid. 5 They go to the mosque. 6 They hug their friends. **4** free answers

Page 30–31 **1** 1 king 2 baby 3 present 4 candy 5 shoe 6 tree **2** 1 Twelfth Night is in January. 2 It's 12 nights after Christmas. 3 Three good people gave presents to Jesus. 4 Some people eat a cake on Twelfth Night. 5 Twelfth Night is a big festival in Spain. 6 Spanish children find presents in shoes. **3** 1 Christian 2 Christmas 3 Spain 4 parades 5 costumes 6 shoes **4** 1 Eid 2 Twelfth Night 3 Twelfth Night 4 Twelfth Night 5 Eid 6 Twelfth Night **5** 1 king 2 tree 3 present 4 streets

Page 32–33 **1** 1 season 2 sunny 3 flowers 4 cherry 5 spring 6 picnics **2** 1 true 2 false 3 false 4 false 5 true 6 true **3** free answers **4** free answers

Page 34–35 **1** 1 crown 2 wheat 3 harvest 4 wreath 5 turkey 6 pumpkin pie **2** 1 November 2 wheat 3 family 4 Chuseok 5 girl **3** 1 USA 2 South Korea 3 Italy 4 Poland **4** 1 in the fall 2 farmers 3 South Korea 4 in September or October 5 They eat traditional food and they dance. 6 the USA and Canada 7 in November

Page 36–37 **1** 1 birthday 2 tree 3 teacher 4 sometimes 5 statues 6 birds **2** 1 Guru Nanak's birthday is a Sikh festival. 2 Vesak Day is a Buddhist festival. 3 Christmas is a Christian festival. 4 Eid is a Muslim festival. **3** 1 Guru Nanak was a great teacher. 2 His birthday is in November. 3 Some people go to the Golden Temple. 4 This temple is in India. 5 There are lots of lamps at the temple. **4** free answers

Page 38–39 **1** 1 bonfire 2 flowers 3 lake 4 river 5 pole 6 leaves **2** 1 The days are long in summer. 2 The longest day is called Midsummer. 3 This is a big festival in Sweden. 4 People make big bonfires. 5 It doesn't get dark in Finland. 6 In Russia, girls make pretty crowns. **3** 1 false 2 true 3 false 4 true 5 true **4** free answers

Page 40–41 **1** 1 lantern 2 candy 3 eye 4 nose 5 mouth 6 spider **2** 1 When is Halloween? It's on October 31st. 2 What is a Halloween lantern made of? It's made of a pumpkin. 3 What is the day after Halloween? It's All Saints Day. 4 Where is All Saints Day a big festival? It's big in Mexico. 5 Is All Saints Day a sad festival? No, it isn't. **3** 1 lanterns 2 costumes 3 pumpkins 4 aren't 5 spiders **4** 1 Children wear costumes at Halloween. 2 They knock on doors. 3 People give children candy. 4 People aren't really scared. 5 People have fun on All Saints Day. 6 They play with their brothers and sisters.

Page 42–43 **1** 1 true 2 true 3 true 4 false 5 true 6 false **2** 1 different things 2 twelve 3 like 4 Thailand 5 hot **3** 1 candle 2 parade 3 bonfire 4 skeleton 5 fireworks 6 present 7 wheat 8 pumpkin **4** free answers

3 Free Time Around the World

Subject Area

The World of Arts & Social Studies

Topics & Curriculum Links

sports and other free-time activities (Civics)
countries (Geography)
climate and the environment (Geography)
musical instruments (Music)
quantities and measurements (Mathematics)

Vocabulary

sports; hobbies; weather; transportation; clothes; parts of the body; musical instruments; numbers; months; seasons; places; countries

Grammar

present simple; past simple; question forms; imperative; adjectives; prepositions

Teaching Ideas

See also pages 6–7 for general ideas that you can adapt. Or go to **www.oup.com/elt/teacher/readanddiscover**

Land, Water, and Air Activities

After reading Chapter 9, in small groups or as individuals, students complete a chart like the one on page 40 of the Reader, listing all the land, water, and air activities that they can think of. Or they can write an activity for each letter of the alphabet. They then share their ideas with the class, and collect all the ideas on the board.

READ & TALK Free-Time Activities

After completing Project 1, students do a survey to find out what activities the whole class does. They can do this by listening to each student giving information in turn, or by collecting the class information in a big chart on the board. Then they make a bar chart showing the different activities, and the number of students that do them, to find the most popular activity. They can talk or write about the chart like this: *The most / least popular free-time activity is ... A lot of / some / a few students do / play ... The favorite activity for girls / boys is ...*

Free-Time Fact Files

Students do research, using books or the Internet, about a free-time activity in their country. Then they write about it and display the information with pictures. They can write about it like this: [Activity] *started in ... You need ... You wear ... It's ...* Students can then present their free-time activity to the class.

Sports Around the World

Students do research, using books or the Internet, about sports around the world. They can choose a sport and find out where in the world it is popular, or they can choose a country and find out what sports are popular there. They display their findings on a poster with pictures, and they can label a copy of the world map on page 7. Students can work in groups, and posters can then be displayed together.

Activities Answers

Pages 24–25 **1** 1 pitch 2 ball 3 player 4 team 5 boots **2** 1 popular 2 street 3 boots 4 five 5 sand **3** 1 soccer 2 futsal 3 soccer 4 futsal 5 futsal 6 futsal **4** 1 Soccer is a very popular sport 2 People like watching and playing soccer 3 You don't need expensive boots. 4 Many Brazilian children play futsal. 5 There are five players in a futsal team. 6 The futsal ball is full of sand.

Pages 26–27 **1** 1 tobogganing 2 skiing 3 snowboarding 4 dog sledding **2** 1 sunny 2 cloudy 3 windy 4 hot 5 cold 6 warm **3** 1 colder 2 colder 3 hotter 4 hotter **4** 1 Skiing, tobogganing and dog sledding 2 There's a big dog sled race. 3 No, you can't. 4 It is hot outside the snow dome. 5 free answer 6 free answer

Pages 28–29 **1** 1 India 2 always 3 fast 4 colorful 5 is 6 movies **2** 1 bindi 2 earring 3 bangles 4 necklace **3** 1 In India there are many different types of dance. 2 Bollywood dance is popular all around the world. 3 Bollywood dance is fast and colorful. 4 Bollywood makes about 1,000 movies every year. 5 Bollywood dancers wear colorful clothes and jewelry. **4** free answers

Pages 30–31 **1** 1 false 2 false 3 true 4 true 5 false 6 false **2** 1 back kick 2 side kick 3 flying side kick 4 jumping back kick **3** 1 white 2 yellow 3 green 4 blue 5 red 6 black **4** 1 About 70 million people practice tae kwon do. 2 Students learn different moves with their hands and feet. 3 Students wear different-colored belts to show their level. 4 The black belt is the last belt. 5 In Taeglish lessons students learn tae kwon do and English.

Pages 32–33 **1** 1 book 2 newspaper 3 story 4 magazine 5 comic book **2** 1 true 2 false 3 true 4 false 5 true 6 true **3** 1 science fiction 2 comedy 3 magazine 4 adventure 5 cartoon 6 book **4** free answers

Pages 34–35 **1** 1 team 2 cheerleaders 3 court 4 gymnastics **2** 1 fast 2 gardens 3 is 4 team 5 3; 6 isn't **3** 1 basketball 2 cheerleading 3 basketball 4 cheerleading 5 basketball **4** 1 Many students are in college basketball teams. 2 You can play basketball in a garden. 3 It's fun to watch basketball on television. 4 Cheerleaders are good at dance and gymnastics.

Pages 36–37 **1** 1 pipe (other) 2 bell (percussion) 3 rattle (percussion) 4 drum (percussion) 5 trumpet (other) **2** 1 life 2 times 3 singing 4 instruments 5 plants **3** free answers

Pages 38–39 **1** 1 surfing (water) 2 snorkeling (water) 3 swimming (water) 4 kayaking (water) 5 volleyball (sand) 6 cricket (sand) **2** 1 false 2 true 3 true 4 false 5 false 6 true **3** 1 Volleyball and cricket 2 On some beaches, and also in the desert 3 free answer

Pages 40–41 **1** sailing (water), walking (land), skateboarding (land), paragliding (air), camping (land), snorkeling (water), kayaking (water), climbing (land) **2** 1 1907; 2 11, 18; 3 6, 25; 4 28; 5 216 **3** 1 It started in 1907. 2 The first Scouts were boys from 11 to 18 years old. 3 They learned how to read maps and make fires. 4 Anyone from 6 to 25 years old can be a Scout. 5 free answer

Pages 42–43 **1** 1 Cycling 2 good 3 paths 4 85% 5 bicycles **2** 1 cycling 2 BMX 3 BMX 4 cycling **3** 1 BMX riding is popular in many countries. 2 There are two types of BMX riding. 3 You can do BMX racing around a track. 4 The best place to practice BMX freestyle is in a skatepark. **4** 1 free answers

4 All About Plants

Subject Area

The World of Science & Technology

Topics & Curriculum Links

plant classification (Science)
plant parts (Science)
a plant life cycle (Science)
photosynthesis (Science)
plants in the environment (Science; Geography)
plants in danger (Geography, Civics)
animals (Science)
plant materials (Science; Technology)
sizes and measurements (Mathematics)
first plants: plant fossils (History; Science)

Vocabulary

plants; plant parts; food; weather; places; animals; materials; numbers; measurements

Grammar

present simple; present continuous; past simple; question forms; imperative; adjectives; prepositions; adverbs

Teaching Ideas

See also pages 6–7 for general ideas that you can adapt. Or go to **www.oup.com/elt/teacher/readanddiscover**

READ & TALK A Plant Presentation

After completing Project 2, students present their plant poster to the rest of the class. They can write or talk about their plant like this: *The plant is called ... The fruit is called ... / The vegetable is from the root / stem / leaf / flower. It comes from [Countries]. The flower is ... The leaf is ...* Students can then display all the posters together, organizing them into fruit and vegetables, or by different types of plant.

READ & TALK An Amazing Plants Quiz

Choose one of the plants from the Reader, and without saying its name, read out one fact about it and ask students to guess which plant it is. Read out more facts, one at a time, until students guess the correct plant. You can use a point scoring system, for example, five points after one fact, three points after two facts, etc. Students can then do this in small groups or pairs.

READ & TALK What Is in the Photo?

Using the photo on page 18 of the Reader, students list the objects – those made of plant materials and then the others. Then in pairs they can play a game where one student chooses an object in the photo and the other student has to guess what it is. The first student can describe it, or the second student can ask questions. They can also do the same activities with objects in the classroom.

Plant Parts

Using a bigger version of the chart on page 29 of the Reader, students list as many examples as possible. They can do research or limit it to plants that they know.

Activities Answers

Pages 24–25 **1** Plants: They keep growing; Plants and Animals: They are living things. They feed. They breathe. They grow. Animals: They move from place to place. They don't grow when they are older. **2** 1 There were no plants or animals. 2 The first plants grew in water. 3 The first plants grew on land. 4 There were animals on Earth. **3** 1 two billion 2 300,000 3 hundreds of millions 4 400 million **4** 1 true 2 false 3 true 4 true 5 false 6 true **5** Plants can breathe, grow, and make new plants.

Pages 26–27 **1** 1 Seed plants: flowering plants, conifers; non-seed plants: ferns, mosses **2** 1 seeds 2 don't make 3 seeds 4 flowers 5 non-seed **3** 1 They aren't seeds, but new plants grow from them: spores 2 It makes seeds, but it doesn't produce flowers: conifer 3 It produces flowers: flowering plant 4 It doesn't make seeds: non-seed plant 5 Most plants make them: seeds **4** 1–5 free answers

Pages 28–29 **1** 1 flower 2 leaf 3 stem 4 roots **2** 1 Roots take water from the soil. 2 Stems support the plant. 3 Leaves make food for the plant. 4 Flowers make seeds. 5 New plants grow from the seeds. 6 Seeds are in the fruit. **3** 1 Leaves: cabbage; Stems: asparagus; Flowers: broccoli; Roots: potato; Fruits: apple **4** 1 The main parts are leaves, stems, roots, and flowers. 2 The roots. 3 The stems. 4 Lots of parts. 5 Seeds 6 free answers

Pages 30–31 **1** 1 seeds 2 flowers 3 pollen 4 fruit 5 pollination 6 water **2** 1 false 2 true 3 true 4 true 5 false **3** 1 water 2 male 3 pollination 4 seeds 5 fruit **4** 1 seed 2 plant 3 flowers 4 insects 5 grow 6 fruit

Pages 32–33 **1** 1 glucose 2 oxygen 3 water 4 carbon dioxide 5 sunlight. Plants use: sunlight, carbon dioxide, water; Plants make: glucose, oxygen **2** 1 Plants can make their own food. 2 Plants use sunlight to make glucose. 3 During photosynthesis plants produce oxygen. 4 Photosynthesis happens in leaves. 5 In the leaves there is chlorophyll. 6 The chlorophyll catches the sunlight. **3** 1 food 2 sunlight 3 use 4 change 5 winter

Pages 34–35 **1** 1 shade 2 quickly 3 cold 4 flowers 5 shelter **2** 1 arctic buttercup 2 cactus 3 sea grass 4 cactus 5 cactus 6 sea grass **3** cactus: dry, top, water, stem; arctic buttercup: cold, small, ground; sea grass: underwater, pollinate **4** 1 In very dry, cold, or wet places, or in places where there isn't much sunlight. 2 Because its roots are near the top of the ground. 3 To help the flowers live in the wind and the cold. 4 The waves.

Pages 36–37 **1** 1 colors 2 bird 3 bee 4 pollen 5 fly 6 smell **2** 1 Plants produce food for animals to eat, and oxygen for them to breathe. Animals also make their homes in or around plants. 2 Animals pollinate flowers. 3 Because they can see some colors better than others. **3** 1 oxygen 2 pollinate 3 nectar 4 colored 5 patterns 6 sweet **4** Bees like: yellow and blue, sweet smells; Flies like: light colours, smells like meat; Birds like: red, no smell

Pages 38–39 **1** 1 clothes 2 chair 3 eraser 4 door 5 table 6 book 7 fire 8 medicine **2** 1 true 2 false 3 true 4 true 5 false 6 false **3 Example answers** Wood: chair, floor, table; Paper: book, poster; Cotton: clothes, bag **4** 1–4: free answers

Pages 40–41 **1** 1 smelliest 2 eats 3 tallest 4 smallest 5 roots 6 2,000 **2** 1 About every six years. 2 It has traps with very small hairs. 3 Six million. 4 On water. **3** 1 The titan arum is a very smelly plant. It smells like bad meat. 2 The coast redwood is a very tall plant. It can grow to 110 meters tall. 3 The wolffia is a very small plant. It's less than a millimeter long. 4 The Venus flytrap is an insect-eating plant. It eats insects. **4** Free answers

Pages 42–43 **1** 1 airport 2 habitat 3 rainforest 4 roads 5 trees 6 crops 7 pollution **2** 1 When people build new roads, they cut down plants. 2 There are lots of palm oil farms in the rainforest. 3 Pollution puts chemicals into the soil. 4 Chemicals are bad for plants. **3** 1 **Example answer** They produce oxygen. 2 **Example answer** They are cut down so people can grow crops to sell. **4** 1 free answers

4 How to Stay Healthy

Subject Area
The World of Science & Technology

Topics & Curriculum Links
human body; how the body works (Science)
healthy food and drink; food types (Science)
sports and exercise (Civics; Science)
life at home (Civics)
healthy lifestyle; protecting your body (Science; Civics)
disabilities (Science; Civics)
microbes; personal hygiene (Science; Civics)
sizes, measurements, and quantities (Mathematics)
places and countries (Geography)

Vocabulary
food and drink; sports; activities; parts of the body; transportation; numbers; measurements; places; countries; continents

Grammar
present simple; present continuous; past simple; question forms; imperative; adjectives; prepositions; adverbs

Teaching Ideas

See also pages 6–7 for general ideas that you can adapt. Or go to **www.oup.com/elt/teacher/readanddiscover**

My Plate of Food
After reading Chapter 3, students collect pictures of food that they eat. Then they make a poster of their own version of the food plate, to show what they eat, and how much of each food type they usually eat. They can also add food labels to the pictures.

READ & TALK Food Around the World
After reading Chapter 4, students do more research on traditional dishes and/or food from a country of their choice, using books or the Internet. Then they can make a poster and present their findings to the rest of the class. Students then display all the posters together. They can organize the information by continent or country.

READ & TALK An Exercise Survey
After completing Project 2, students collect the survey information from the class. They can do this by listening to each student giving their information in turn, or by collecting the information in a big chart on the board. Then they make a bar chart to show the class results.

How to Stay Healthy Posters
Students make posters about how to stay healthy. Students can work in groups, and each group can focus on a different aspect, for example, food and drink, exercise, protecting your body. Posters can then be displayed together.

Activities Answers

Page 24–25 **1** 1 body 2 healthy 3 medicines 4 exercise 5 fast 6 food **2** 1 medicines 2 outdoors 3 disabilities 4 body 5 exercise 6 healthy 7 travel **3** 1 true 2 false 3 true 4 true 5 true 6 false **4** free answers

Page 26–27 **1** 1 brain 2 lungs 3 heart 4 liver 5 intestines 6 bone 7 skin 8 muscle 9 kidneys 10 stomach **2** 1 It moves blood around your body – heart 2 It breaks down the food that you eat – stomach 3 It makes different parts of your body work well – brain 4 It protects your body – skin 5 They support your body – bones 6 They help you to breathe - lungs **3** 1 blood 2 breathe 3 bones 4 liver, kidneys 5 temperature 6 move **4** 1 true 2 true 3 false 4 false 5 true 6 false

Page 28–29 **1** 1 fruit 2 milk 3 bread 4 fish 5 vegetables 6 rice **2** 1 Carbohydrates: bread; Proteins: fish, meat, eggs; Vitamins: fruit, vegetables **3** 1 proteins 2 fat 3 sugar 4 calcium 5 vitamins 6 fiber **4** 1 Carbohydrates give your body energy. 2 Fiber helps food to move through your stomach and intestines. 3 Proteins help your muscles to grow. 4 You need calcium for healthy bones. 5 Too much fat, sugar, and salt is unhealthy.

Page 30–31 **1** 1 Peru 2 Bolivia 3 China 4 Japan 5 Mediterranean Sea **2** 1 fruit 2 vegetables 3 salad 4 rice 5 fish 6 meat 7 bread 8 olive oil **3** 1 rice 2 fat 3 salad 4 quinoa 5 chopsticks 6 tomatoes 7 iron **4** free answers

Page 32–33 **1** 1 Millions 2 sick 3 food 4 toilet 5 dirty 6 meat **2** 1 in your mouth 2 microbes 3 dentist 4 sugar **3** 1 false 2 true 3 true 4 true 5 true **4** 1 millions 2 Wash your hands. 3 The microbes on your teeth eat the sugar, too. 4 To keep them healthy. 5 Go to the dentist; don't eat too much food with sugar.

Page 34–35 **1** 1 bones, muscles 2 problems 3 good 4 work 5 healthy **2** 1 Everyone needs to do exercise to stay healthy. 2 Exercise isn't only for young, healthy people. 3 You need to do some exercise every day. 4 Swimming is a good exercise, and most people can do it. 5 Many people with disabilities can do team sports and athletics. 6 You don't have to go to the sports center every day. **3** 1 Everyone needs to do exercise to stay healthy. 2 Exercise protects you from health problems. 3 Exercise isn't only for young people. 4 Swimming is a good exercise. 5 You can play sports in the park. 6 Exercise helps you to work better at school. **4** free answers

Page 36–37 **1** 1 lungs 2 breathe 3 heart 4 blood 5 food 6 sweat **2** 1 breathe 2 lungs 3 heart 4 blood 5 skin 6 cool down **3** 1 need 2 faster 3 more healthy 4 can't 5 short 6 bigger **4** 1 Because your lungs take in more air to give your body more oxygen. 2 It cools down your skin when it dries. 3 oxygen 4 Your muscles can't get all the oxygen that they need. 5 Walking, jogging, cycling, swimming 6 running fast

Page 38–39 **1** 1 walk 2 skip 3 jog 4 stretch **2** 1 Before exercise: Warm up your muscles; do stretching exercises 2 When you do exercise: Breathe slowly and deeply 3 After exercise: Cool down your muscles; do more stretching exercises; drink **3** 1 muscles 2 arms, legs 3 breathe 4 cool down 5 equipment 6 lights **4** 1 walk, jog, skip 2 run slowly, walk 3 (Use the right equipment to) protect your head and body; wear bright clothes; use lights.

Page 40–41 **1** 1 cycling 2 walking 3 team sports 4 adventure sports **2** 1 happier 2 school 3 walking 4 sun 5 teeth, bones 6 suncream **3** 1 It's good to spend time outdoors. 2 Some people do exciting adventure sports. 3 The sun can damage your skin. 4 It's important to wear suncream. 5 What sports do you do outdoors? 6 Your skin uses the sun to make Vitamin D. **4** free answers

Page 42–43 **1** 1 rest 2 grow 3 muscles 4 sleep 5 brain 6 repair **2** 1 true 2 false 3 true 4 true 5 false **3** 1 protein 2 repair 3 hard 4 brain 5 good, healthy **4** 1 Small pieces of protein in your muscles break. 2 So that your brain can rest. 3 Between six and eight hours every night. **4–5** free answers

Subject Area

The World of Science & Technology

Topics & Curriculum Links

materials and components (Science; Technology)
machines in the environment (Geography)
machines that help people (Technology; Civics)
sizes and measurements (Mathematics)
energy and fuel (Science)
places and countries (Geography)
dates and events (History)

Vocabulary

machines; tools; materials; transportation; buildings; weather; fuel; computer parts; numbers; measurements; dates; places; countries

Grammar

present simple; past simple; future simple; question forms; imperative; adjectives; prepositions; adverbs

Teaching Ideas

See also pages 6–7 for general ideas that you can adapt. Or go to **www.oup.com/elt/teacher/readanddiscover**

READ & TALK Big and Small

After reading Chapter 10, students do research, using books or the Internet, about more very big and very small machines. Then they write about their machines and display the information with pictures. They can use the models in Chapter 10, for example: *It's a / an ... It's ... meters high / long. It has ... It weighs ... It's smaller / bigger than a ...* Students can present their machines to the class.

READ & TALK A Machine Presentation

After completing Project 2, students present their machine to the rest of the class. They can write and talk about their machine like this: *This machine is called a / an ... The machine can ... It's for ... It's made of ... [Name] invented it in ...* Or other students can ask the questions on page 45 of the Reader. Students can then display all the machine posters together. They can put the machines in chronological order, maybe with a time line, to show when the machines were invented or first used.

Machines Research

Students choose a material, for example, wood, stone, metal. Or they choose a part, for example, lever, ramp, pulley. Then they do research, using books or the Internet, about machines and the material or part chosen. They then present their findings on a poster.

Activities Answers

Pages 24–25 **1** 1 stone 2 wood 3 bone 4 metal **2** 1 stone and wood. 2 stone and bone. 3 wood. 4 wood. 5 stone and bone. 6 wood. **3** 1 machines 2 wood 3 farming 4 plows 5 levers 6 tools **4** 1 People used bows to shoot arrows. 2 They built canals to get water for their plants. 3 They used levers to move heavy objects like rocks. 4 People started making metal tools about 5,000 years ago.

Pages 26–27 **1** 1 wheel 2 clay pot 3 rollers 4 axle 5 cart 6 car **2** 1 People used rollers to move heavy objects. 2 An axle is a bar that connects two wheels. 3 Potters used wheels to make clay pots. 4 The London Eye is a very big wheel. 5 Carts and chariots are vehicles with wheels. **3** 1 false 2 true 3 true 4 false 5 false **4** 1 vehicle 2 wheelchair 3 skateboard 4 bicycle 5 chariot 6 rollers

Pages 28–29 **1** 1 temple 2 rope 3 pulley 4 block 5 ramp 6 crane **2** 1 ramps 2 blocks 3 workers 4 cranes 5 pulleys 6 ropes **3** 1 They help us to lift objects more easily. 2 They needed many workers, because the blocks were very heavy. 3 They used rollers to move the blocks up the ramps. 4 The biggest pyramid in Egypt is at Giza. 5 The biggest pyramid is 138 meters high. **4** 1 used 2 tied 3 put 4 lifted 5 pulled 6 needed

Pages 30–31 **1** 1 watermill 2 sail 3 arm 4 millstone 5 wheel 6 axle 7 river 8 windmill **2** 1 true 2 true 3 false 4 true 5 false 6 false **3** 1 flour 2 water 3 wheel 4 axle 5 wind 6 sails 7 arms 8 grain **4** 1 has 2 works 3 turns 4 breaks 5 pushes; the secret word is: nature

Pages 32–33 **1** 1 water clock 2 digital clock 3 mechanical clock 4 sand clock 5 sundial **2** 1 Sundial: pointer, sun; Water Clock: pots, water; Sand Clock: glass bubbles, sand; Mechanical Clock: pendulum, gears, springs; Digital Clock: batteries **3** 1 true 2 false 3 true 4 true 5 false 6 false **4** digital, sand, mechanical, clock, shadow, bubble, sundial, numbers, batteries, spring

Pages 34–35 **1** 1 bus 2 plane 3 car 4 train 5 helicopter 6 boat 7 diesel 8 wood 9 gasoline 10 oil 11 biodiesel 12 coal **2** 1 Buses can travel long distances. true 2 Today many vehicles use wood. false 3 Electric cars use energy from batteries. true 4 Trains and planes use human energy. false 5 Biodiesel is made from plant materials. true **3** 1 Most vehicles use gasoline or diesel. 2 Electric cars don't produce smoke or pollution. 3 Bicycles use human energy. 4 free answer

Pages 36–37 **1** 1 plane 2 propeller 3 hot-air balloon 4 helicopter 5 jet engine 6 airship **2** 1 Hot-air balloons are slow and hard to control. 2 Helicopters can be useful in emergencies. 3 Some planes have powerful jet engines. 4 Planes didn't exist 200 years ago. **3** 1 false 2 true 3 false 4 false 5 true **4** 1 freight 2 propellers 3 engine 4 passengers 5 hospital 6 helicopter; the secret word is: flight

Pages 38–39 **1** 1 telephones, sounds 2 televisions, images 3 Radios, wires 4 cell phones, messages 5 satellites, programs **2** 1 John Logie Baird invented the first television in 1926. 2 Guglielmo Marconi invented the radio in 1895. 3 Inventors invented the color television in 1944. 4 Alexander Graham Bell invented the telephone in 1876. **3** communicate, photo, wire, message, screen, radio, sound, image, transmit, invent, satellite, program **4** free answers

Pages 40–41 **1** 1 speaker 2 monitor 3 cursor 4 printer 5 modem 6 headphones 7 keyboard 8 joystick 9 mouse **2** 1 big 2 30; 3 expensive 4 1980; 5 Web **3** 1 watch movies 2 print documents 3 play games 4 type words 5 click on buttons 6 use the Internet 7 listen to music **4** 1 The *ENIAC* computer was built in about 1946. 2 The *ENIAC* computer cost about 500,000 dollars. 3 Tim Berners-Lee invented the World Wide Web, or the Web. 4 We can move the cursor with a mouse. 5 free answer

Pages 42–43 **1** 1 96, 240, 13,500; 2 1.7, 4.8, 180; 3 65, 360, 5,400; **2** 1 cruise ship 2 mining machine 3 microscopic 4 passenger 5 vehicle 6 scientists **3** 1 true 2 false 3 false 4 true 5 true 6 false 7 true 8 false **4** 1 The *Bagger* is a mining machine. 2 They will use nanobots to help people who are sick. 3 The *Oasis* has three swimming pools. 4 & 5 free answers

Subject Area

The World of Science & Technology

Topics & Curriculum Links

materials and products (Science; Technology)
recycling waste (Science; Technology)
pollution; dangers for the environment (Geography; Civics)
life at home (Civics)
protecting the environment (Science; Civics)
quantities and measurements (Mathematics)

Vocabulary

materials; everyday objects; food; numbers; measurements; places

Grammar

present simple; present continuous; question forms; imperative; adjectives; prepositions; adverbs

Teaching Ideas

See also pages 6–7 for general ideas that you can adapt. Or go to **www.oup.com/elt/teacher/readanddiscover**

Things That We Can Recycle

After completing Project 1, students share their ideas with the class, and make a list of all the things that we can recycle. They can complete a chart like the one on page 42 of the Reader. They list all the things made of plastic, paper, glass, or metal.

READ & TALK A Recycling Survey

After completing Project 2, students collect the survey information from the class. They can do this by listening to each student giving their information in turn, or by collecting the information in a big chart on the board. Then they make a bar chart to show the class results.

READ & TALK Recycling in My Home

Students find out what happens to the food waste, plastic waste, paper waste, etc. in their home. Then they write a short report using language like this: *In my home, the food waste goes to a recycling factory / landfill. The ... waste goes to ...* Students then report back to the rest of the class, and they can compare findings.

Recycling Posters

Students design posters to promote recycling in their school. Students then display all the posters together, and they can vote for their favorite poster. The winning poster can be copied and displayed around the school.

Activities Answers

Page 24–25 **1** 1 countries, five, day 2 big 3 fast 4 slowly 5 never 6 less **2** 1 plastic, up to 1,000 years 2 glass, never 3 some metals, from 80 to 100 years 4 paper, from 2 to 5 months **3** 1 landfill 2 waste 3 5 kilograms 4 waste 5 never 6 months 7 years 8 less **4** free answers

Page 26–27 **1** 1 When we reduce our waste, we make less waste. 2 When we reuse our waste, we use it again. 3 When we recycle our waste, we use it to make something new. 4 We should put less waste in landfills. 5 We can fix things when they break. **2** 1 false 2 true 3 true 4 false **3** 1 reuse 2 reduce 3 recycle 4 use **4** 1 recycle 2 reuse 3 reduce 4 waste 5 landfill 6 elephant 7 glass 8 metal 9 plastic 10 paper; odd one out: elephant **5** free answers

Page 28–29 **1** 1 batteries 2 television 3 computer 4 shoes 5 cans 6 clothes **2** 1 recycle 2 clear 3 many 4 symbols **3** 1 recycle 2 new 3 glass 4 colors 5 plastic 6 good 7 cars **4** 1 There's a recycling symbol. 2 cans, cars, computers 3 No, but we can recycle most things.

Page 30–31 **1** 1 newspaper 2 paper recycling factory 3 newspaper factory **2** 1 paper 2 factory 3 machines 4 fibers 5 ink 6 glue 7 staples 8 trees 9 soap 10 air **3** 1 false 2 true 3 true 4 false **4** 1 Paper is made from ~~cars~~ trees. 2 When we recycle ~~chocolate~~ paper, we save trees. 3 At a paper recycling factory, machines cut the paper and put the pieces in ~~pizzas~~ water. 4 Machines wash paper fibers to take out things like ~~dogs~~ staples and ~~cats~~ glue. 5 Every time we recycle paper, the fibers get ~~bigger~~ smaller and ~~stronger~~ weaker. 6 We will always need some new ~~bottles~~ trees to make paper. **5** free answers

Page 32–33 **1** 1 car 2 chair 3 phone 4 refrigerator 5 bottle 6 toys **2** 1 decompose 2 different 3 bottles 4 clothes 5 factory **3** 1 Plastic is newer than other materials. 2 There aren't many factories that recycle plastic. 3 We can recycle plastic from things like bottles. 4 Different factories recycle different types of plastic. 5 We can use recycled plastic to make clothes. **4** 1 They clean the plastic. 2 They cut the plastic into small pieces. 3 They melt the plastic. 4 They clean the plastic again. 5 They cut the clean plastic into pellets.

Page 34–35 **1** 1 blow 2 hot 3 sand 4 magnet 5 melt 6 machine **2** 1 Glass is made from sand. 2 People sort the glass into different colors. 3 Machines break the glass into small pieces. 4 When we make new glass from recycled glass we can save energy. 5 People can recycle glass again and again. 6 We use most recycled glass to make new glass things. **3** 1 false 2 true 3 true 4 false 5 true 6 false **4** 1 sand 2 energy 3 materials 4 recycled 5 factory, pieces

Page 36–37 **1** 1 metals 2 aluminum 3 energy 4 rocks 5 hot 6 bar **2** 1 different 2 rocks 3 energy 4 recycle **3** 1 We save energy when we recycle metals. 2 We recycle different metals in different ways. 3 Aluminum is the metal in most drinks cans. 4 We can recycle all metals. 5 Aluminum bars are very big. **4** 1 They come from rocks. 2 Because we can recycle it again and again. 3 They are made from aluminum. 4 by melting metal 5 more than one million

Page 38–39 **1** 1 We can't eat banana skins. 2 In landfills food decomposes very slowly. 3 We can reduce waste when we only buy the food that we need. 4 We can make compost with our food waste. 5 Compost helps plants to grow. **2** free answers **3** 1 false 2 false 3 true 4 true 5 true 6 true **4** 1 food 2 banana 3 garden 4 decomposes 5 compost; secret word: farms

Page 40–41 **1** 1 Glass is made from sand. 2 Paper is made from trees. 3 Plastic is made from oil. 4 Metal comes from rocks. **2** 1 oil 2 trees 3 yellow 4 problems 5 pollution 6 factories 7 energy 8 waste; odd one out: yellow **3** 1 plastic 2 future 3 waste 4 animals **4** 1 Landfills 2 is 3 kill 4 can 5 machines 6 new **5** 1 factories, landfills, waste 2 They can kill plants and animals. 3 So that we can have them in the future.

Page 42–43 **1** 1 For plastic: cars, plastic bottles, plastic boxes; For paper: newspapers, birthday cards; For glass: glass bottles; For metal: cars, cans, computers **2** 1 You can reduce your ~~schools~~ waste. 2 Borrow a computer game from a ~~cat~~ friend. 3 Fix things when they ~~sing~~ break. 4 ~~Write~~ Make things from waste. **3** 1 reduce 2 reuse, recycle 3 reuse 4 reduce 5 recycle **4** 1 reduce 2 reuse 3 recycle 4 waste 5 plastic 6 metal 7 glass 8 paper **5** free answers

4 All About Desert Life

Subject Area

The Natural World

Topics & Curriculum Links

deserts and the environment (Science; Civics)
deserts around the world (Geography)
plants and animals (Science)
life at home (Civics)
seasons, weather, and climate (Geography)
places and countries (Geography)
desertification (Science; Geography)
quantities and measurements (Mathematics)

Vocabulary

plants; animals; food; materials; homes; weather; seasons; transportation; numbers; measurements; places; countries; continents

Grammar

present simple, present continuous; past simple; question forms; imperative; adjectives; prepositions; adverbs

Teaching Ideas

See also pages 6–7 for general ideas that you can adapt. Or go to **www.oup.com/elt/teacher/readanddiscover**

A Desert Advert

After completing Project 1, students design an advert for their desert, listing what people can see and do there, and also listing what they should bring on their trip, for example, water, suncream, sun glasses, a hat. Posters can then be displayed together.

READ & TALK A Desert Animal Presentation

After completing Project 2, students present their animal to the rest of the class. They can talk or write about it like this: *It's a / an ... It's ... It lives ... It eats ... It comes out ...* Or students can talk about their animal without saying its name, and ask the class to guess the animal. Posters can then be displayed together.

Desert Research

Using books or the Internet, students do research on how plants, animals, or people adapt to desert life. They can write about their findings and add pictures. They can write about it like this: *To stay cool ... To collect water ...*

Activities Answers

Page 24–25 **1** 1 snow 2 rain 3 mountain 4 stones 5 sand 6 rocks **2** 1 25 2 50 3 0 4 2, 4 5 5 **3** 1 false 2 true 3 true 4 false 5 true 6 false **4** 1 Some deserts have no rain for months or years. 2 Deserts can be hot or cold. 3 The temperatures in hot deserts are from 20 to 35 degrees centigrade. 4 At night it's cold in the desert. 5 The winter temperatures in cold deserts are from 2 to 4 degrees centigrade. 6 Water in cold deserts comes from snow or fog.

Page 26–27 **1** 1 nine 2 Africa 3 hot 4 Mongolia 5 coldest 6 one desert **2** 1 Gobi 2 Sahara 3 Gobi 4 Atacama 5 Sahara 6 Atacama **3** 1 desert 2 sand dunes 3 sandstorms 4 coldest 5 rock **4** 1 One of the oldest deserts is the Atacama Desert. 2 180 metres tall 3 in Peru and Chile 4 minus 40 degrees centigrade 5 the USA 6 1,300,000 square kilometres

Page 28–29 **1** 1 leaves 2 soil 3 spikes 4 stem 5 seeds 6 roots **2** 1 Cactus: spikes, water; Baobab: desert, 9 meters; Welwitschia: leaves, fog **3** 1 dry 2 big 3 store 4 grow 5 soil 6 fog **4** 1 So it can collect water fast when it rains. 2 They collect water, and they stop animals eating the plant. 3 thousands of liters 4 more than 9 meters across 5 the leaves 6 They grow fast and produce flowers.

Page 30–31 **1** 1 true 2 true 3 false 4 true 5 true 6 false **2** 1 Insects: ant; Mammals: jerboa; Arachnids: spider, scorpion; Reptiles: snake, lizard **3** 1 ant (2) 2 snake (1) 3 spider (4) 4 scorpion (5) 5 tortoise (6) 6 lizard (3) **4** 1 seeds 2 poison 3 plants 4 skin 5 bigger 6 tortoises

Page 32–33 **1** 1 Animals that come out in the day: lizards, desert tortoises, many birds; Animals that come out at night: foxes, scorpions, desert cats, owls **2** 1 in the day 2 at night 3 in the day 4 at night 5 in the day 6 at night **3** 1 food 2 see 3 well 4 hairs 5 feel **4** 1 Lizards lie on rocks to get warm. 2 Tortoises look for food in the morning 3 Most desert animals sleep in the day. 4 Small animals sleep in burrows. 5 Scorpions have tiny hairs on their legs. 6 Desert cats can see well at night.

Page 34–35 **1** 1 mud house 2 wood 3 tent 4 farm 5 city 6 clothes **2** 1 clothes 2 things 3 art 4 farmers 5 2,000 6 first **3** 1 Aborigines live in the Australian deserts. 2 Many aborigines are going back to their traditional life. 3 Tuaregs are called the blue people. 4 Tuareg tents are made from animal skins and wood. 5 Many Bedouins work in cities. **4** 1 Because of the color of their clothes. 2 on camels 3 They use art. 4 tents or mud houses 5 in cities

Page 36–37 **1** 1 oasis 2 river 3 pond 4 well 5 tank 6 lake **2** 1 true 2 false 3 false 4 true 5 false 6 true **3** 1 dry 2 ground 3 farming 4 collect 5 rainwater 6 fog **4** 1 in Egypt 2 in ponds, wells, and big tanks 3 They use nets to collect it. 4-5 free answers

Page 38–39 **1** 1 People wear long clothes to stay cool. 2 People wear a head cloth to protect their head and face. 3 Some desert houses have no windows. 4 The houses keep out the sun and the wind **2** 1 Oryxes 2 Crocodiles, snakes 3 tortoises 4 lizards 5 hole 6 clothes **3** 1 Many people and animals live in deserts. 2 Desert people use clothes to stay cool. 3 Some desert houses have no windows. 4 Big animals stay in a cool place. 5 Some animals sleep in summer. 6 Some lizards can swim under the sand. **4** 1 a head cloth 2 So that it stays cool inside. 3 Stay in a cool place in the day. 4 They swim under the sand.

Page 40–41 **1** 1 porridge 2 bread 3 cheese 4 dates 5 milk **2** 1 false 2 false 3 true 4 false 5 true 6 false **3** 1 fires 2 cheese 3 sand 4 tents 5 SUVs 6 schools **4** free answers

Page 42–43 **1** 1 plants 2 animals 3 tree 4 rain 5 farm 6 soil **2** 1 true 2 true 3 false 4 true 5 true **3** 1 desert 2 rain 3 blows away 4 food 5 hungry **4** 1 When there's no rain for a long time. 2 There isn't food for everyone. 3 In countries in Africa near the Sahara Desert. 4 By growing more trees.

4 All About Ocean Life

Subject Area
The Natural World

Topics & Curriculum Links
oceans and the environment (Science; Civics)
oceans around the world (Geography)
plants and animals (Science)
food chains (Science)
classification (Science)
parts of the body (Science)
sizes and measurements (Mathematics)

Vocabulary
oceans; animals; plants; places; food; parts of the body; numbers; seasons; measurements

Grammar
present simple; present continuous; past simple; question forms; imperative; adjectives; prepositions; adverbs

Teaching Ideas

See also pages 6–7 for general ideas that you can adapt. Or go to **www.oup.com/elt/teacher/readanddiscover**

READ & TALK An Ocean Animal
After completing Chapter 4 and the activity on page 31 of the Reader, students present their animal to the class, without saying its name. They can talk about it like this: *It's a mammal / fish / bird. It eats ... It lives ... It has ... It's ... It can ...* Students then guess which animal it is. Or students ask questions, for example: *Is it a mammal / fish / bird? What does it eat? Where does it live? How big is it? What does it look like?* Students can also do this with other ocean animals from the Reader.

Oceans in Danger Posters
After completing Project 1, students choose one of the dangers and make a poster about it. Students can work in groups, and posters can then be displayed together.

Ocean Research
Using books or the Internet, students do research on oceans, for example, to find out the size of oceans, the countries near them, the islands in them, or which animals live there. They can write about their findings and add pictures. They can also use a copy of the world map on page 7.

Activities Answers

Pages 24–25 **1** 1 Arctic Ocean 2 Pacific Ocean 3 Atlantic Ocean 4 Indian Ocean 5 Southern Ocean **2** 1 five 2 70; 3 two 4 30; 5 two **3** 1 ocean 2 Arctic 3 warmer 4 coral reefs 5 waves 6 biggest 7 water **4** 1 blue whale 2 Arctic 3 Southern 4 currents 5 tides

Pages 26–27 **1** 1 plant plankton 2 animal plankton 3 small fish 4 dolphin 5 great white shark **2** 1 Dolphins eat small fish. 2 Great white sharks eat dolphins. 3 Whale sharks eat plankton. 4 Sea otters eat sea urchins. **3** 1 They are very small animals and plants. 2 Because they need sunlight. 3 A predator is an animal that eats other animals. 4 The biggest fish in the world is the whale shark. 5 Kelp is seaweed. **4** free answer

Pages 28–29 **1** 1 sea anemones 2 mangrove trees 3 limpets 4 shellfish **2** 1 animals, seashore 2 low tide 3 rocks 4 shell 5 salt 6 tentacles, dry out **3** 1 Ocean Animals: sea anemones, sharks, animal plankton, limpets, sea urchins, shrimps, sea otters, whales; Ocean Plants: mangrove trees, plant plankton, kelp **4** 1 a limpet 2 a sea anemone 3 a mangrove tree 4 a shark 5 plankton

Pages 30–31 **1** 1 milk 2 flippers 3 blowhole 4 two hours 5 eggs 6 bigger wings **2** Mammals: sea lion, sperm whale, blue whale, dolphin; Birds: albatross; Fish: shark **3** free answers

Pages 32–33 **1** 1 shark 2 lionfish 3 clownfish 4 sea anemone 5 sea urchin 6 cleaner wrasse **2** 1 They are small animals with hard covers: corals 2 They sting predators with their tentacles: sea anemones 3 They live near the tentacles of sea anemones: clownfish 4 They have spines that can sting: lionfish 5 They clean other fish: cleaner wrasse **3** 1 false 2 false 3 true 4 true 5 false 6 false **4** 1 colors 2 camouflaged 3 skin 4 kill 5 mouths

Pages 34–35 **1** 1 octopus 2 shoal of fish 3 porcupine fish 4 leafy sea dragon 5 starfish 6 seaweed **2** 1 It grows a new arm: a starfish 2 It turns a different shape so that nothing can eat it: a porcupine fish 3 It makes a cloud of black ink: an octopus 4 It hides in seaweed: a leafy sea dragon 5 They swim together in big groups: a shoal of fish 6 It turns a different color: an octopus **3** 1 They are called shoals. 2 It looks like seaweed. 3 They camouflage themselves by turning a different colour. 4 They make a big cloud of black ink. 5 It drinks lots of water. 6 It gets big and round like a ball. **4** free answers

Pages 36–37 **1** shark 2 nostril 3 teeth 4 jellyfish 5 tentacles 6 angler fish 7 light 8 head 9 eye **2** 1 prey 2 head 3 television 4 tentacles 5 dark 6 head **3** 1 It gives fish an electric shock: electric ray 2 It can see and smell all around: hammerhead shark 3 It stings fish with its tentacles: jellyfish 4 It has a light on its head so other fish swim near: angler fish **4** free answers

Pages 38–39 **1** 1 bird 2 polar bear 3 seal 4 penguin 5 whale 6 dolphin **2** 1 a lot of 2 summer 3 biggest, small 4 food 5 South 6 feet **3** 1 polar bears: **any three from** They live in the Arctic, Most of the year they live on ice, They catch seals from holes in the ice, They swim between the ice and icebergs, They are the biggest type of bear, Their cubs are very small **plus free answer;** penguins: **any three from** They live near the South Pole, They dive into the ocean for fish and other small animals, They have special feathers that keep them warm and dry, Their feathers sometimes make them too hot, They keep their eggs on their feet **plus free answer**

Pages 40–41 **1** 1 fish 2 pearls 3 ice cream 4 seaweed 5 oysters **2** 1 false 2 true 3 false 4 false 5 true 6 true **3** 1 oysters 2 shell 3 ropes 4 Pearls 5 money; 3, 2, 5, 4, 1; 6 grows 7 collects 8 dries 9 sells 10 put; 9, 8, 6, 7, 10

Pages 42–43 **1** 1 oil 2 chemicals 3 plastic bags 4 fishing nets 5 Marine parks **2** 1 Because birds and other animals eat it and it gets onto their skin or feathers, and it can kill them. 2 Because they look like jellyfish when they're in the water and sea turtles eat them. 3 Sometimes, they catch dolphins, sea turtles, seals, and birds. **3** Pollution: dirty water and chemicals, people leave things on beaches, oil; Fishing: big nets catch animals, fishermen take too many fish; Damage: boats break coral reefs **4** 1 There are new rules so people can't take too many fish from the ocean. 2 There are new types of fishing net, which big animals can swim out of. 3 There are marine parks where the ocean is always clean and safe.

Subject Area

The Natural World

Topics & Curriculum Links

animals (Science)

animals senses (Science)

parts of the body (Science)

places and environments (Geography)

animal migrations (Science)

quantities and measurements (Mathematics)

Vocabulary

mammals, fish, minibeasts, birds; parts of the body; senses; food; weather; numbers; measurements; places; continents

Grammar

present simple; present continuous; question forms; imperative; adjectives; prepositions; adverbs

Teaching Ideas

See also pages 6–7 for general ideas that you can adapt. Or go to **www.oup.com/elt/teacher/readanddiscover**

READ & TALK Nocturnal Animals

After completing Project 1, students present their animal to the rest of the class. They can talk or write about it like this: *It's a / an ... It's ... It has ... It lives ... In the day, it ... At night, it ...* Or students can talk about their animal without saying its name, and ask the class to guess the animal. Posters can then be displayed together.

READ & TALK Guess the Animal

Choose one of the animals from the Reader, and without saying its name, read out one fact about it and ask students to guess which animal it is. Read out more facts, one at a time, until students guess the correct animal. You can use a point scoring system, for example, five points after one fact, three points after two facts, etc. Students can then do this in small groups or pairs.

Nocturnal Animals in My Country

Using books or the Internet, students do research on nocturnal animals on their own country. They find out what these animals do in the day, how well they see and hear and how they find food. They can display their findings in a chart like the one on page 28 of the Reader.

Activities Answers

Page 24–25 **1** 1 In the day: nocturnal animals sleep, hotter, light; At night: dark, nocturnal animals don't sleep, colder **2** 1 Armadillos come out at night. 2 Tigers come out in the day and at night. 3 Rabbits come out in the morning and in the evening. 4 Opposums come out at night. **3** 1 false 2 false 3 false 4 true **4** 1 hides 2 nocturnal 3 evening 4 predator **5** 1 not so many 2 more 3 hot

Page 26–27 **1** 1 Raccoons have long fingers and a good sense of touch. 2 Foxes have big ears and a good sense of hearing. 3 Tarsiers have big eyes and a good sense of sight. 4 Foxes have big noses and a good sense of smell. **2** 1 tarsier 2 fox 3 raccoon 4 mice 5 frogs **3** 1 taste 2 12 3 Raccoons 4 big 5 light 6 brain **4** 1 Many nocturnal animals have special senses. 2 Wild dogs usually hunt in the dark. 3 Raccoons use their fingers to find food. 4 Nocturnal animals can see better than people. 5 Tarsiers can see well in the dark.

Page 28–29 **1** 1 Food: Owls – rabbits, mice, and other small animals; Bats – fruit, flowers, insects, fish, and mice. Where they stay in the day: Owls – in trees or buildings; Bats – in caves, trees, or buildings. Special senses: Owls – can see well in the dark, amazing sense of hearing; Bats – can see and smell very well, use echolocation. Another amazing fact: Owls – have soft feathers on their wings to help them fly quietly; Bats – are the only mammals that can fly. **2** 1 bat 2 owl 3 owl 4 bat 5 bat **3** 1 sharp claws 2 prey 3 soft feathers 4 wing **4** 1 They listen for little noises from their prey. 2 in their sharp claws 3 Because they have soft feathers on their wings. 4 echolocation 5 Where things are and how big they are.

Page 30–31 **1** 1 Plankton are small animals that are food for fish. 2 Lantern fish are fish that have lights on their body when they swim. 3 Whitetip reef sharks are fish that stay in caves in the day. **2** 1 Plankton are very ~~big~~ small animals. 2 They swim ~~down to the deep~~ up to the top of the ocean at night. 3 Lantern fish stay at the ~~top~~ bottom of the ocean in the day. 4 In the day, the whitetip reef shark ~~feeds~~ stays in caves. **3** 1 night 2 evening 3 day 4 lights **4** 1 They eat fish and octopuses. 2 To look for plankton. 3 They eat plankton. 4 Near the top of the ocean. 5 It hunts for fish and octopuses.

Page 32–33 **1** 1 moth 2 spider 3 slug 4 snail 5 firefly **2** 1 sun 2 antennae 3 patterns 4 hairs 5 poison 6 lights **3 Example answers** Moths: 1 They are insects. 2 They have a body that's good for living at night. 3 They have special antennae on their head; they have patterns on their wings; (and free answers). Tarantulas: 1 They are spiders. 2 They hunt for their prey at night. 3 They have special hairs on their body, they use poison; (and free answers). **4** 1 Because there are not so many predators that hunt and eat them. 2 They help them to look for food and to find their way in the dark. 3 patterns on their wings 4 at night

Page 34–35 **1** 1 fennec fox 2 ears 3 kangaroo rat 4 legs 5 scorpion 6 tail **2** 1 false 2 true 3 true 4 true 5 false 6 true **3** 1 in a burrow in the sand 2 mice, lizards, and insects 3 They keep them in their mouth, and then they put them in their burrow. 4 with a sting from their tail **4** 1 seeds, kangaroo rat 2 hairs, scorpion 3 smallest, fennec fox 4 ears, fennec fox 5 water, kangaroo rat 6 see, scorpion

Page 36–37 **1** 1 aardvark 2 bushbaby 3 leopard 4 hippo **2** 1 ears, nose 2 seeing, hearing, smell 3 insects, flowers, seeds, eggs **3** 1 cooler 2 insects 3 grass 4 trees 5 tongue 6 tapetum **4** 1 bushbaby 2 hippo 3 aardvark 4 leopard 5 ants

Page 38–39 **1** 1 A baboon sleeps on cliffs or in the tops of trees. 2 A flamingo sleeps standing on one leg. 3 A walrus sleeps with its tusks over pieces of ice. **2** 1 ten 2 ankles 3 nineteen 4 air 5 tusks **3** 1 Because they are safe from predators. 2 They stand on one leg. 3 They have special ankles. 4 on land, on ice, or in water 5 They put lots of air in their special pouches. 6 Because they put their tusks over big pieces of ice. **4** free answers

Page 40–41 **1** 1 owl 2 lion 3 deer 4 nightingale 5 grasshopper 6 Tasmanian devil 7 howler monkey **2** 1 Owls call to each other at night. 2 Most birds do not sing at night. 3 The male nightingale sings for a female. 4 The Tasmanian devil makes terrible noises. **3** 1 A deer hits the ground with its ~~nose~~ feet when it's in danger. 2 A grasshopper makes noises with its wings and ~~mouth~~ legs. 3 A Tasmanian devil is a ~~big~~ small animal that hunts for food in the dark. 4 You can hear howler monkeys from about ~~10~~ 5 kilometers away. **4** 1 Deer make noises in their nose when they are in danger. 2 Nightingales sing when they are looking for a female. 3 Tasmanian devils make terrible noises when they are scared.

Page 42–43 **1** 1 true 2 true 3 false 4 true **2** 1 beach 2 eggs 3 baby 4 ocean **3 Example answers** 1 Because they are safer from predators, and they can fly for longer because it's cooler. 2 Not usually, but they travel at night when they are ready to lay their eggs. 3 in the sand on a beach 4 Because it's cooler, and there are not so many predators. **4** 1 Desert animals: scorpion, fennec fox; Ocean animals: green turtle, plankton; African animals: aardvark, hippo; Animals that fly at night: owl, bat.

4 Incredible Earth

Subject Area

The Natural World

Topics & Curriculum Links

environments around the world (Geography)
places and countries (Geography)
sizes and measurements (Mathematics)
dates and events (History)
physical processes (Geography)
animals (Science)
dangers from the environment (Geography; Civics)

Vocabulary

places; materials; animals; weather; transportation; numbers; measurements; countries; continents

Grammar

present simple; present continuous; past simple; question forms; imperative; adjectives; prepositions; adverbs

Teaching Ideas

See also pages 6–7 for general ideas that you can adapt. Or go to **www.oup.com/elt/teacher/readanddiscover**

Incredible Places Around the World

After completing Project 2, students do research, using books or the Internet, about incredible places in another country, or about a type of place. They display their findings on a poster with pictures, maps, charts, etc. Students can write about their places like this: *This is [Name] ... It's a [type of place] ... It's in [Country] ...* It's incredible because ... Students can work in groups, and posters can then be displayed together.

READ & TALK An Incredible Tour

Using the information from the Reader and/or information from books or the Internet, students plan a tour of five or ten incredible places around the world. They can use a copy of the world map on page 7 to show their tour. They can write and talk about it like this: *First, we're going to visit ... in ... It's a ... We're going to see ... Then ... Next ... After that ... Finally ...* Then they can present their tour to the rest of the class, or all the tours can be displayed together. Then students can vote for the best tour.

Activities Answers

Pages 24–25 **1** 1 Earth is round. 2 Earth's crust is millions of years old. 3 The pieces of Earth's crust move very slowly. 4 There are different rocks in Earth's crust. 5 Under Earth's crust, there's very hot rock. 6 There are volcanoes under the ocean. **2** 1 old 2 crust 3 holes 4 volcano 5 ocean 6 rocks **3** 1 crust 2 Earth 3 earthquake 4 island 5 mountain 6 ocean 7 rocks 8 volcano **4** 1 Earth 2 skin 3 piece 4 volcano 5 ground 6 desert

Pages 26–27 **1** 1 valley 2 waves 3 cliffs 4 coral 5 sea turtle 6 dolphin **2** 1 true 2 false 3 true 4 true 5 false 6 true **3** 1 It's the Pacific Ocean. 2 It's 10 kilometers deep. 3 They are in Bali in Indonesia. 4 It's made of millions of very small animals. 5 It's near Australia. **4** 1 The Pacific Ocean is bigger than Africa. 2 There are big mountains under the ocean. 3 When waves hit the land, rocks fall into the ocean. 4 Coral is hard, but it isn't made of rock. 5 Many amazing animals live near coral reefs.

Pages 28–29 **1** 1 mountain 2 waterfall 3 rainforest 4 river **2** 1 South America 2 hard 3 mountains 4 through 5 anaconda **3** 1 kilometer 2 rock 3 snake 4 mountain 5 Amazon **4** 1 ocean 2 Amazon 3 rainforest 4 Brazil 5 Iguazu Falls 6 anaconda **5** 1 The water in rivers comes from rain or snow. 2 When a river goes over rocks, it makes waterfalls AND/OR rapids. 3 Iguazu Falls is a South American waterfall. 4 The Amazon begins in the mountains in Peru. 5 The Amazon goes through a big rainforest. 6 You can find snakes in the Amazon.

Pages 30–31 **1** 1 glacier 2 mountain 3 slowly 4 icebergs 5 ice 6 incredible **2** Hot: Amazon Rainforest, coral reef, volcano, melted rock; Cold: glacier, ice, iceberg, snow **3** 1 Glaciers move very slowly. 2 Glaciers are rivers made of ice. 3 Icebergs are dangerous for boats. 4 Ilulissat is one of the coldest places. **4** 1 When do glaciers begin? They begin when snow falls. 2 What are glaciers made of? They are made of ice. 3 Why are icebergs dangerous? Because most of the ice is under the water. 4 Where is Ilulissat? It's near the North Pole. 5 How long is the glacier at Ilulissat? It's about 40 kilometers long.

Pages 32–33 **1** 1 rain 2 snow 3 geyser 4 pool 5 steam 6 waterfall **2** 1 true 2 false 3 false 4 false 5 true 6 true **3** 1 Under a geyser there is a lot of hot rock. 2 Geysers make a loud noise. 3 The water in a geyser is very hot. 4 Don't go near a geyser. 5 The cliffs at Pamukkale look like waterfalls. 6 Pamukkale is in Turkey. **4** 1 Deep under the ground, there is hot rock. 2 When water boils, it makes steam. 3 The monkeys at Jigokudani sit in the warm water. 4 In the water there are minerals. 5 The cliffs at Pamukkale look like waterfalls. 6 Don't go near geysers because they are very hot.

Pages 34–35 **1** 1 mountain chain 2 moved 3 slowly 4 highest 5 deepest 6 rivers **2** 1 water 2 rainforest 3 mountain 4 top 5 very 6 Earth **3** 1 What is the highest mountain in the world? Mount Everest. 2 What is the deepest lake in the world? Lake Baikal. 3 What is the biggest mountain chain in the world? The Himalayas. 4 What is the biggest river in the world? The Amazon. **4** free answers

Pages 36–37 **1** 1 near 2 move 3 caves 4 Borneo 5 rock 6 pictures **2** 1 Caves are usually wet. 2 Limestone is a soft rock. 3 There are often caves in limestone. 4 People drew pictures on cave walls. 5 Now most people don't live in caves. **3** 1 Where is the Sarawak Chamber? It's in Borneo. 2 Is limestone very hard? No, it's soft. 3 Are caves usually wet? Yes, they are. 4 What are stalactites made of? They are made of rock. 5 Why did people draw on cave walls? Because they didn't have books or paper. 6 Do you like caves? free answer

Pages 38–39 **1** 1 earthquake 2 flood 3 building 4 tsunami 5 tree 6 wave 7 house 8 ocean **2** 1 moves 2 buildings 3 under 4 ocean 5 in **3** 1 false 2 true 3 true 4 false 5 true 6 false **4** 1 Earth's crust moves a few millimetres every year. 2 Big earthquakes are very dangerous. 3 Earthquakes under the ocean sometimes make tsunamis. 4 A tsunami is a giant wave. 5 After a tsunami, there are often floods.

Pages 40–41 **1** 1 sand 2 stones 3 salt 4 rocks 5 rain 6 lake 7 desert 8 ground **2** 1 Some deserts are made of sand. 2 It doesn't rain often in Antarctica. 3 The Sahara Desert is bigger than Australia. 4 Animals in the desert don't drink very often. 5 In Bolivia, there is a desert made of salt. 6 The Salar de Uyuni is an incredible place. **3** 1 Deserts are usually hot. 2 Deserts are very dry places. 3 The Sahara Desert is in Africa. 4 It's very cold in Antarctica. 5 Many people visit the Salar de Uyuni. **4** 1 How much of the land on Earth is desert? About 20 percent. 2 What is the biggest hot desert on Earth? The Sahara Desert. 3 Where is Bolivia? In South America. 4 Why do many people visit the Salar de Uyuni? Because it's an incredible place.

Pages 42–43 **1** 1 Where is Cappadocia? It's in Turkey. 2 What changed the rocks in Cappadocia? The wind changed them. 3 Where is the Grand Canyon? It's in the USA. 4 What is the name of the river in the Grand Canyon? It's called the Colorado River. 5 When did erosion begin in the Colorado River? About 20 million years ago. **2** 1 water 2 earthquakes 3 desert 4 caves 5 volcano 6 Australia 7 lake 8 glacier 9 geyser 10 ocean **3** free answer

4 Animals in Art

Subject Area

The World of Arts & Social Studies

Topics & Curriculum Links

paintings, drawings, sculptures, and other types of art (Art)
colors and shapes (Art; Technology)
materials (Science; Technology)
animals (Science)
parts of the body (Science)
places and countries (Geography)
dates and events (History)
quantities and measurements (Mathematics)

Vocabulary

animals; colors; parts of the body; senses; shapes; materials; numbers; measurements; places; countries; continents

Grammar

present simple; present continuous; past simple; question forms; imperative; adjectives; prepositions; adverbs

Teaching Ideas

See also pages 6–7 for general ideas that you can adapt. Or go to **www.oup.com/elt/teacher/readanddiscover**

READ & TALK A Favorite Picture Survey

After completing Project 1, students collect the votes for the favorite picture. They can do this by listening to each student giving their information in turn, or by collecting the information in a big chart on the board. Then they make a bar chart to present the results of the vote.

READ & TALK An Animal in Art

After completing Project 2, students present their animal in art to the rest of the class. They can talk or write about it like this: *This is called ... It's a [type of art]. The artist is ... The artist made it in [date]. It shows ...* Students then display all the posters together, organizing them by type of art, or type of animal. Then they can vote for their favorite animal in art.

READ & TALK Which Picture Is It?

Choose a picture from the Reader, and ask students to guess which picture it is. Describe it to the class without saying which page it's on, for example: *It's a [type of art]. There's a ... It's ... It has ...* Then ask students to do the same in pairs, taking turns to describe a picture.

Activities Answers

Page 24–25 **1** 1 artist 2 dog 3 painting 4 cat 5 fur 6 drawing **2** 1 can't 2 run 3 fly 4 Cats 5 fur 6 soft **3** free answers **4** 1 Most insects can fly. 2 Cats can climb trees. 3 Most cats have soft fur. 4 Many artists draw pictures of animals. 5 Animal shapes are different from ours.

Page 26–27 **1** 1 bison 2 spider 3 giraffe 4 plane 5 desert 6 cave **2** 1 false 2 true 3 false 4 false 5 true **3** 1 People painted animals on the walls of caves. 2 A Spanish girl discovered the cave paintings at Altamira. 3 There's a big picture of a monkey in the Nazca Desert 4 Some pictures in the Nazca Desert are bigger than a playground. 5 There are paintings of giraffes in a cave in Libya. **4** 1 Altamira is in Spain. 2 A girl called María Sanz de Sautuol discovered them. 3 It's in Peru. 4 They drew monkeys, birds, and spiders. 5 giraffes and other animals 6 about 8,000 years old

Page 28–29 **1** 1 British 2 French 3 mountains 4 jungle 5 stag 6 tiger **2** 1 Are you from Spain? Yes. I'm Spanish. 2 Are you from South Korea? Yes. I'm Korean. 3 Are you from Poland? Yes. I'm Polish. 4 Are you from the USA? Yes. I'm American. 5 Are you from England? Yes. I'm English. 6 Are you from Russia? Yes. I'm Russian. **3** 1 Whales live in the ocean. 2 Stags live in the mountains. 3 Polar bears live in the Arctic. 4 Camels live in the desert. 5 Tigers live in the jungle.

Page 30–31 **1** 1 boy 2 bird 3 India 4 animal 5 pet 6 emperor **2** free answers **3** 1 Artists sometimes paint people with their pets. 2 Francisco de Goya was a Spanish artist. 3 The boy in the painting has a black and white bird. 4 The boy's cats are watching his bird. 5 The rabbit is made of snow. 6 The dog has a short tail. **4** 1 Francisco de Goya was a Spanish artist. 2 He painted lots of portraits. 3 He painted a boy and his pets. 4 The boy has a black and white bird. 5 He also has two cats. 6 The cats are watching the bird.

Page 32–33 **1** 1 was 2 museum 3 10 4 Spain 5 statue 6 tall **2** 1 in Canada 2 a sculpture of a spider 3 in Barcelona in Spain 4 wood 5 in Alert Bay in Canada **3** 1 taking 2 making 3 painting **4** 1 He's making a sculpture of a lion. 2-3 free answers

Page 34–35 **1** 1 Internet 2 drawings 3 lots 4 realistic 5 drew 6 birds **2** 1 true 2 false 3 false 4 true 5 false **3** 1 A long time ago, people didn't have televisions. 2 They looked at pictures of animals in books. 3 Some artists drew pictures in children's books. 4 The rabbit on page 14 is wearing clothes. 5 *Alice's Adventures in Wonderland* is about a girl called Alice. 6 Do you like watching animals on television? **4** 1 A long time ago, people looked at animals in books. 2 Today we can watch animals on television. 3 *Alice's Adventures in Wonderland* is a children's book. 4 The rabbit on page 14 is looking at his watch. 5 Do you like the birds on page 15? 6 John Audubon was a good artist.

Page 36–37 **1** 1 snake 2 rooster 3 sheep 4 rabbit 5 tiger 6 monkey 7 horse 8 dog **2** 1 pictures 2 France 3 stamps 4 symbol 5 people **3** 1 The bull is the symbol of Spain. 2 The kangaroo is the symbol of Australia. 3 The bear is the symbol of Russia. 4 The eagle is the symbol of the USA. 5 The tiger is the symbol of South Korea. **4** free answers

Page 38–39 **1** 1 horse 2 Brancusi 3 painting 4 realistic 5 marble 6 photo **2** 1 artist 2 Romania 3 seal 4 realistic 5 idea 6 hard 7 stone 8 table **3** 1 Franz Marc was a German painter. 2 He painted a picture of three animals. 3 The colors in his painting are not realistic. 4 The elephant's head is red. **4** 1 Seals live in the ocean. 2 They can swim fast. 3 Franz Marc was a German painter. 4 His painting of animals isn't realistic. 5 Constantin Brancusi was from Romania. 6 Do you like his sculpture?

Page 40–41 **1** 1 monkey, 4 2 shape, 2 3 wheels, 3 4 lion, 1 **2** 1 teapot 2 toy 3 bird 4 hedgehog **3** 1 The teapot on page 20 is in the shape of a zebra. 2 The toys on page 21 are about 3,000 years old. 3 It's fun to look at sculptures of animals. 4 Some old toys have wheels. **4** 1 Look! It's a teapot in the shape of a zebra. 2 It's by an American artist. 3 These old toys are from Iran. 4 We don't know the artist's name. 5 Maybe they're the oldest toys in the world. 6 You usually can't touch sculptures in a museum.

Page 42–43 **1** 1 tail 2 eye 3 horn 4 wing 5 body 6 head 7 mouth 8 claw **2** 1 three on each foot 2 a dragon with five claws 3 white 4 No, there aren't. 5 yes 6 free answers **3** 1 cats: painting, page 5 2 seal: sculpture, page 18 3 spider: sculpture, page 12 4 giraffe: cave painting, page 7 5 lizard: statue, page 13 6 zebra: sculpture, page 20 7 rabbit: photo & painting, page 3; drawing, page 14 8 unicorn: tapestry, page 23 9 stag: painting, page 8 10 sheep: sculpture, page 17 11 dog: drawing, page 4 12 tiger: painting, page 9 13 monkey: giant picture, page 7 14 dragon: picture, page 22 15 birds: drawing, page 15

4 Wonders of the Past

Subject Area

The World of Arts & Social Studies

Topics & Curriculum Links

types of building (Technology)
materials (Science; Technology)
places and countries (Geography)
sizes and measurements (Mathematics)
dates and events (History)
architecture (Art)
sports and other hobbies (Civics)
animals (Science)

Vocabulary

buildings; materials; places; animals; hobbies; transportation; measurements; dates; numbers; countries

Grammar

present simple; past simple; question forms; imperative; adjectives; prepositions; adverbs

Teaching Ideas

See also pages 6–7 for general ideas that you can adapt. Or go to **www.oup.com/elt/teacher/readanddiscover**

READ & TALK A Wonders Survey
After completing the last activity for each chapter, students collect the wonders star ratings from the class. They can do this by listening to each student giving their star ratings in turn, or by collecting the information in a big chart on the board. Then they calculate how interesting / beautiful / important the class thinks each wonder is by adding up the stars. Then they make a bar chart, and they can talk or write about the results like this: *... people in our class think that ... is the most beautiful / interesting / important wonder.*

READ & TALK A Wonders Quiz
After completing Project 1, students make up their own version of the quiz and try it out on the class.

READ & TALK Wonders Posters
After completing Project 2, students present their wonder to the rest of the class. They can talk or write about it like this: *The wonder is called ... It's in ... It's made of ... It's ... years old.* Students then display the posters together. Students can also research other wonders from around the world, using books or the Internet. They can also create a timeline to display the wonders posters in chronological order. Students can then vote for the best wonder.

READ & TALK Secret Wonders
Choose a wonder from the Reader, then describe it to the class without saying its name: *It's in ... It's a ... It's made of ... It's ... years old.* Or ask students to guess the wonder by asking questions, for example: *Where is it? What is it? What's it made of? How old is it?* Then ask students to do the same in pairs, taking turns to describe a wonder. They can also do this for wonders from their own country.

Activities Answers

Pages 24–25 1 1 sun 2 mountain 3 stars 4 stone 5 circle **2** 1 kilometer 2 metric ton 3 year 4 cemetery 5 study 6 mystery **3** 1 5,000 2 45 3 250 4 80 5 4,000 **4** 1 They came from mountains 250 kilometers away. 2 As a cemetery, or a place for studying the sun and the stars, or as a temple. 3 June 21st. **5** free answers

Pages 26–27 1 1 bed 2 mask 3 jewel 4 tomb 5 coffin 6 king **2** 1 He was a king (more than 3,300 years ago). 2 He lived in Egypt. 3 He was only 19 years old. **3** Treasures: boats, jewels, masks; Places: Valley of the Kings, Cairo, Egypt; People: Tutankhamun, Egyptians, Howard Carter **4** king, tomb, valley, mask, king, coffin, jewels, statue, tomb, door, tomb. **5** free answers

Pages 28–29 1 1 wall 2 tower 3 bricks 4 prisoner 5 soldier 6 war 7 moon **2** 1 friends, enemies 2 build, destroy 3 high, low 4 long, short 5 live, die **3** 1 countries 2 enemies 3 years 4 soldiers 5 hard 6 stone, bricks **4** 1 often 2 sometimes 3 sometimes 4 never **5** free answers

Pages 30–31 1 1 rhino 2 gladiator 3 lion 4 elephant 5 crocodile 6 arch **2** 1 Romans 2 stadium 3 animals 4 arches 5 roof 6 city **3** 1 500,000 2 1,000,000 3 80 4 50,000 **4** 1 They went to watch fights. 2 Gladiators and wild animals. 3 To let people in and out. 4 Two earthquakes. 5 To build other buildings. **5** free answers

Pages 32–33 1 1 The caravans stopped at Petra because it had water and places to sleep. 2 The palaces and tombs are built in the cliffs. 3 The caravans used camels to transport people and things. 4 People carried cloth and spices to sell in different places. 5 Earthquakes destroyed a lot of Petra, but you can still see some of it today. **2** 1 spices 2 movies 3 cliff 4 stone 5 earthquake 6 camel 7 cloth 8 palace 9 theater 10 caravan **3** free answers

Pages 34–35 1 1 statue 2 ocean 3 island 4 head 5 ground 6 coast **2** They grow: people, plants, animals, trees; Things that we do: push over, fight, cut down, transport **3** 1 In the Pacific Ocean 2 It has 887 stone statues. 3 1,700 years ago. 4 Lots of plants and animals. 5 Big statues for their gods. **4** free answers **5** free answers

Pages 36–37 1 1 well 2 ground 3 dry 4 pyramid 5 games 6 dance **2** 1 well 2 water 3 god 4 pyramids 5 games 6 dance **3** 1 in the past 2 today 3 in the past 4 in the past 5 today **4** 1 About 1,600 years ago. 2 The rain god. 3 The Temple of Kukulkan. 4 They played ball games. **5** free answers

Pages 38–39 1 1 city 2 rainforest 3 rain 4 enemies 5 trees 6 monkeys 7 rich 8 mountain **2** 1 false 2 true 3 true 4 false 5 true 6 false **3** 1 The king wanted a new temple. 2 People built the temple. 3 It became rich and powerful. About one million people lived there. 4 There were wars. 5 People visit it. **4** free answers **5** free answers

Pages 40–41 1 1 tower 2 garden 3 tourist 4 fountain 5 tiles 6 wall **2** 1 tree 2 ground 3 plant 4 old 5 prisoner 6 story **3** 1 water, fountain 2 tower, castle 3 plants, garden 4 tiles, Alhambra 5 decorations, walls **4** 1 In the mountains in the south of Spain. 2 It is a castle. 3 About 800 years ago. 4 In the courtyards. 5 Wars and an earthquake. **5** free answers

Pages 42–43 1 1 People: wife, Shah Jahan, son, emperor, Mumtaz Mahal, father, baby; Things: tomb, fountain, jewels, stones, garden, palace, prison **2** 1 Mumtaz Mahal died. 2 Shah Jahan wanted to remember his wife. 3 Shah Jahan built the Taj Mahal. 4 Shah Jahan's son wanted to be the emperor. 5 Shah Jahan went to prison. 6 Shah Jahan died. 7 People put Shah Jahan's body in the Taj Mahal. **3** 1 An emperor. 2 About 20,000 people. 3 Elephants **4** 1 ✓ 2 ✓ 3 ✓ 4 ✗ 5 ✗ 6 ✓ 7 ✗ 8 ✓ **5** free answers

Subject Area

The World of Science & Technology

Topics & Curriculum Links

materials and products (Science; Technology)
natural resources (Science)
production processes (Technology)
buildings and construction (Science; Technology, History)
shapes (Technology; Mathematics)
tools and machines (Technology)
energy and the environment (Science; Civics)
electronic products (Science; Technology)
communications (Technology)
future materials (Technology, Science, Civics)
dates and events (History)
sizes and measurements (Mathematics)
places and countries (Geography)

Vocabulary

materials; products; machines; tools; places; buildings; food; clothes; plants; furniture; animals; buildings; transportation; shapes; numbers; measurements; countries

Grammar

present simple; present continuous; past simple; future simple; present perfect; question forms; imperative; passive; adjectives; prepositions; adverbs

Teaching Ideas

See also pages 6–7 for general ideas that you can adapt. Or go to **www.oup.com/elt/teacher/readanddiscover**

READ & TALK A Design for a Home

After reading Chapter 8, students design a home for the future, listing what materials the home is made of. Students present their design to the rest of the class. Designs can then be displayed together, and students write comments on each other's design. Or they can vote for their favorite design.

Products Research

Using books or the Internet, students do research on what materials and products are produced in their country. They can write about their findings like this: Animals: ... *are raised; We use ... to make ...; Plants: ... is/are grown. We use ... to make ...; Materials: ... are produced. We use ... to make ...; Rocks and Minerals: We use ... to make ...*

Activities Answers

Page 36–37 **1** 1 bone 2 fur 3 grass 4 metal 5 wood 6 stone **2** 1 forest 2 flint 3 shelters 4 sticks 5 weaving 6 smelting **3** 1 temples walls/palaces/pyramids 2 clothes/beds/baskets 3 bricks/pottery 4 gold/bronze **4** 1 They used animal fur and grass to make clothes. 2 Animals and fruit and fish. 3 Because it can hold water. 4 About 10,000 years ago 5 By mixing two metals together. 6 Tools and weapons.

Page 38–39 **1** 1 wedges 2 metals 3 Crystals 4 Rubies 5 blast furnace 6 ore **2** 1 copper 2 iron 3 aluminum 4 steel 5 copper 6 aluminum 7 steel 8 copper **3** 1 minerals 2 jewelry 3 electricity 4 liquid 5 cans 6 statue **4** 1 false 2 false 3 false 4 false 5 true 6 false **5 Example answer** During iron smelting, people put iron ore, a chemical called carbon, and a stone called limestone into a very hot place called a blast furnace. At 2,000 degrees centigrade, the carbon and limestone take the other chemicals from the ore, and iron is made. The iron is a hot liquid, and is mixed with other chemicals to make steel.

Page 40–41 **1** 1 fiberglass 2 reinforced 3 skyscraper 4 cement 5 pump 6 grain 7 modern 8 invent **2** 1 skyscrapers, bridges 2 steel, glass 3 glass blower **3** 1 The sand on many beaches is made of cement silica. 2 Glass blowers blow water air through a long, metal tube. 3 People forgot how to make glass concrete for a long time. 4 Fiberglass is made of glass and metal plastic. 5 Concrete becomes hard when fibers crystals grow inside it. 6 The dome of the Pantheon is made of stone concrete. **4** 1 They become darker in the sun and lighter in a room. 2 Because hot and cold don't go through it. 3 Water, sand, and stones. 4 The Ancient Romans 5 1756

Page 42–43 **1** 1 sheep 2 tire 3 cotton 4 curtains 5 boots 6 wool **2** 1 Cotton grows on pants. 2 Farmers collect the cotton. 3 People use machines to collect the cotton. 4 Machines pull the cotton into fibers. 5 Machines spin the cotton fibers into threads. 6 Machines weave threads to make fabric. 7 People make clothes with the fabric. 8 People use dyes to make the fabric different colors. **3** 1 synthetic 2 Oysters 3 pulp 4 spin 5 Dyes 6 cardboard **4** 1 Clothes and curtains. Because it is very soft and warm. 3 When things like grains of sand get into their shells. Rubber balls. **5 free answers**

Page 44–45 **1** 1 gas 2 fuel 3 refinery 4 fertilizer 5 temperature **2** 1 polythene bag 2 fertilizer 3 paint 4 nylon shirt 5 detergent 6 plastic toy **3** 1 plastic, nylon 2 clothes, parachutes 3 toys, plastic bottles **4** 1 We use gasoline to burn as fuel in cars. 2 We use a mold to make plastic shapes/objects. 3 Plastic bags are bad for our world because they take a long time to decompose. 4 Nylon is very strong. We use it to make parachutes. 5 When acrylic paints dry, they become waterproof. **5 Example answers** 1 Oil is made from tiny plants and animals that lived in the seas and oceans millions of years ago. 2 We get different chemicals from oil by heating it until the chemicals become a gas. 3 free answers

Page 46–47 **1** 1 fishing rod 2 Microchips 3 screens 4 properties 5 Firefighters 6 protect **2** 1 Liquid crystal glass is not always transparent. 2 Composite materials are strong and ~~heavy~~ light. 3 Doctors use ~~liquid crystals~~ fiber-optic cables to look inside people's bodies. Silica aerogel is mostly made of ~~water~~ air. **3** 1 parts 2 fiberoptics 3 racket 4 microchips 5 change 6 recycle 7 silicon **4** 1 silicon to make tiny parts for computers 2 aerogels to insulate things 3 composite materials to build planes 4 fiber-optic cables to look inside people's bodies 5 liquid crystals to make pictures on screens **5** 1 To make products that are better. 2 Because we can put millions of electrical parts onto one microchip. 3 To make them stronger to protect people.

Page 48–49 **1** 1 pan 2 oil platform 3 geologist 4 mine 5 pool 6 rocks **2** 1 evaporates 2 drill 3 legs 4 opencast 5 coal 6 miners **3** 1 Explosives are dangerous chemicals that we use in mines. 2 Coal is a mineral that we burn for heat. 3 Radio signals can travel through the ground. 4 Gold is in soil or rocks under the ground. 5 Salt is a mineral that we use in cooking. 6 Soil can have gems or minerals in it. **4** 1 We use machines to measure how electricity and radio signals go through different rocks in the ground and use machines to hit the ground and measure how it moves. 2 Because the water is very deep and the weather can be bad. 3 Because rocks can fall and water and gas can get into the tunnels. 4 They put soil in a pan and wash it with water.

Page 50–51 **1** The Past – fur clothes, bronze weapons, flint tools, grass clothes The Present – fibreglass, concrete, steel, petrochemicals The Future – nanobots, electronic fabric, living homes **2** 1 living 2 furniture 3 button 4 adverts 5 atoms 6 feels **3** 1 electronic clothes 2 nanobots 3 living objects 4 nanobots 5 living objects 6 electronic clothes 7 nanobots **4** 1 They produce waster and dangerous chemicals. 2 Garden furniture. 3 Fiber-optic threads/liquid crystals 4 Tiny tubes, fibers, or balls of atoms. **5** free answers

Subject Area

The World of Science & Technology

Topics & Curriculum Links

history of medicine (Science; History)
types of medicine (Science, History)
parts of the body; inside the body (Science)
healthy lifestyle; keeping clean (Science; Civics)
caring for people and curing illnesses (Science)
medicines made from plants (Science)
medical tools and machines (Technology)
making medicines (Science; Technology)
dates and events (History)
places and countries (Geography)
quantities (Mathematics)

Vocabulary

illnesses; jobs; food; materials; parts of the body; plants; places; buildings; tools; machines; transportation; numbers; countries; continents

Grammar

present simple; present continuous; past simple; future simple; present perfect; question forms; imperative; passive; adjectives; prepositions; adverbs

Teaching Ideas

See also pages 6–7 for general ideas that you can adapt. Or go to **www.oup.com/elt/teacher/readanddiscover**

READ & TALK A Food and Exercise Survey

After completing Project 1, students collect the survey information from the class. They can do this by listening to each student giving their information in turn, or by collecting the information in a big version of the chart on page 52 of the Reader. Then they make a bar chart for each topic (exercise, food, and water), to show the number of people who did what type of exercise, ate what type of food, and drank how much water during the week.

READ & TALK A Medicine Quiz

After completing Project 2, students write more quiz questions. They can work in small groups. Each group writes questions for a different chapter of the Reader, or they can write one question for each chapter. Collect the questions and do the quiz as a whole class.

Activities Answers

Page 36–37 **1** 1 skin 2 wound 3 lotion 4 plants 5 honey 6 bandage 7 mud 8 bone **2** 1 true 2 false 3 true 4 false 5 true 6 true 7 false **3** 1 fever 2 plants 3 lotions 4 medicines 5 skin **4** 1 Ancient Egyptians wrote about their world. 2 They used magic spells and doctors. 3 They used plants. 4 To help wounds to heal. 5 free answers

Page 38–39 **1** 1 India 2 life 3 exercise 4 do yoga 5 Many **2** 1 Acupuncture is a type of medicine. 2 People have used acupuncture for thousands of years. 3 Acupuncture doctors put thin needles into a patient's body. 4 Acupuncture needles stay in the body for up to 30 minutes. 5 No one really knows how acupuncture works. **3** 1 In Ancient Greece, many people believed that angry gods made them ill. 2 Hippocrates told doctors to watch patients and to think about their illnesses. 4 The Olympic Games began because doing sport helped people to stay healthy. **4** 1 Roman 2 toilets 3 baths 4 aqueducts

Page 40–41 **1** 1 hospital 2 prayers 3 plague 4 nuns 5 patients **2** 1 false 2 false 3 true 4 true **3** 1 From about 1,000 years ago barbers started to do surgery. 2 Barbers treated wounds from sword fights. 3 Barbers cut off arms or legs that were badly wounded. 5 The red and white stripes were a symbol for blood and bandages. **4** 1 They are drugs that stop a person feeling pain. 2 They felt a lot of pain. 3 They were made from plants. 4 They rubbed plant medicine into their mouth. 5 Before surgery.

Page 42–43 **1** 1 doctors 2 were not 3 two 4 scientists 5 human bodies **2** 1 Ambroise Pare was an artist about 450 years ago. False 2 At this time, few patients died after surgery. False 3 Ambroise Pare tied blood vessels after he cut off a part of the body. True 4 This stopped many patients dying. True 5 Galen made the first artificial hands, arms, and legs. False 3 1 vein 2 artery 3 lung 4 heart **4** 1 microscope 2 capillaries 3 arteries, veins 4 plaque 5 bacteria

Page 44–45 **1** 1 stop 2 disease 3 weak 4 some 5 cowpox **2** 1 Today, ~~artists~~ doctors and nurses inject vaccines. 2 A vaccine is made from a ~~strong~~ weak type of a virus or bacteria. 3 When a vaccine is inside the body, the body ~~stops~~ starts making antibodies. 4 Antibodies are substances in the ~~hair~~ blood that can kill viruses and bacteria. **3** 1 Louis Pasteur discovered that bacteria in the air could cause disease. 2 Joseph Lister made the first antiseptics. 3 Antiseptics can kill bacteria on tools used in surgery. 5 When we touch things, we get bacteria on our hands. 6 The best way to prevent infections is to wash our hands often! **4** 1 It's an antibiotic. 2 Alexander Fleming, in 1928. 3 It helped thousands of soldiers who were wounded during World War II. It stopped the wounds becoming infected and saved the soldiers' lives.

Page 46–47 **1** 1 pharmacy 2 pills 3 doctor 4 surgeons **2** 1 true 2 true 3 false 4 true 5 true 6 false **3** 1 Malaria is a disease that causes fever and can kill people. 2 People can get malaria when an insect called a mosquito bites them. 3 To cure malaria, people first made a medicine from quinine. 4 Today, quinine drugs are made without plants. 5 Thousands of medicines have been made from rainforest plants. **4** 1 To see if they work and to find out if they are safe. 2 In laboratories. 3 Because making and testing new drugs can take a very long time.

Page 48–49 **1** 1 air ambulance 2 ambulance 3 scanning machine 4 police car 5 X-ray machine **2** 1 body 2 wrong 3 hard 4 bone 5 soft 6 scanning **3** 1 A kidney dialysis machine keeps some patients alive. 2 Kidneys are parts of the body that keep the blood clean. 3 If someone's kidney doesn't work, they can die. 4 A kidney dialysis machine cleans blood and then puts it back inside the body. 5 A pacemaker is a machine that makes a heart work better. 6 Some babies and very young children have pacemakers. **4** 1 When surgeons do keyhole surgery, they ~~listen to the radio~~. watch television. 2 When surgeons do keyhole surgery, they use a ~~large~~ tiny camera. 3 The camera shows on a television screen what is ~~outside~~ inside the patient's body. 4 Surgeons do the operation using long, fat thin tools. 5 Keyhole surgery causes patients ~~more~~ less pain and they get well more quickly.

Page 50–51 **1** 1 medicine 2 vaccine 3 drug 4 surgeon 5 disease 6 cure 7 plants 8 inject 9 robot 10 nanobot **2** 1 false 2 true 3 false 4 true **3** 1 robots 2 nanobots 3 blood 4 body 5 operations 6 scientists 7 medicine **4** free answers

Transportation Then and Now

Subject Area

The World of Science & Technology

Topics & Curriculum Links

transportation (Technology)
materials and components (Science; Technology)
how vehicles work (Science; Technology)
the history of transportation (Science; Geography; History)
trade and industry (Geography; Civics)
sizes and measurements (Mathematics)
energy, fuel and the environment (Science; Civics)
safety (Technology; Civics)
places and countries (Geography)
tourism (Civics Geography)
dates and events (History)

Vocabulary

transportation vehicle parts; materials; fuels; places; weather; animals; measurements; dates; numbers; countries; nationalities; continents

Grammar

present simple; past simple; present perfect; past continuous; future simple; question forms; imperative; passive; adjectives; prepositions; adverbs

Teaching Ideas

See also pages 6–7 for general ideas that you can adapt. Or go to **www.oup.com/elt/teacher/readanddiscover**

READ & TALK What Next?

After reading Chapter 8, ask students to answer the questions: *What transportation will people use in the future? Why? What transportation won't people use very much? Why not?* They can then present their ideas to the class, or they can do this as a class debate.

READ & TALK A Transportation Survey

After completing Project 2, students collect the survey information from the class. They can do this by listening to each student giving their information in turn, or by collecting the information in a big chart on the board. Then they make a bar chart for the results. Students can also do a class survey about how they travel to school. They can talk or write about the results like this: *Most / A lot of / Some / A few people have traveled / travel to school by / in / on [transportation].*

Transportation Research

Students choose a vehicle and do research using books or the Internet, and put the information into a chart like the one on page 45 of the Reader. Or they can display the information on a timeline.

Activities Answers

Pages 36–37 **1** 1 Cart 2 trailer 3 camel 4 spaceship 5 sled 6 ship **2** 1 no 2 yes 3 no 4 yes 5 yes 6 yes **3** Animals: camel, donkey, elephant horse, llama; Vehicles: bicycle, bus, boat, train, truck; Goods: fuel, food, silk, spices, salt **4** 1 People walked or they used animals. 2 Because it's easier to pull heavy things than to lift them. 3 The wheel was one of the most important inventions. 4 Villages and towns became bigger, so people had to travel to find food. 5 It's more than 3,000 kilometers. 6 He flew there in a Russian spaceship.

Pages 38–39 **1** 1 propeller 2 compass 3 oar 4 sail 5 paddle 6 steam engine **2** 1 true 2 false 3 false 4 false 5 true 6 true **3** 1 rafts 2 canoes 3 sailing ships 4 steam ships 5 supertankers **4** 1 Thor Heyerdahl sailed from Peru to an island in the Pacific Ocean. 2 Egyptian sailors sailed on the River Nile. 3 The Ancient Greeks sailed around the Mediterranean Sea. 4 The Vikings lived in Denmark, Sweden, and Norway. 5 The Vikings sailed across the Atlantic Ocean. 6 Traders sailed between Japan, Korea, China, and Southeast Asia. **5** 1 Because they used sails and men rowed with oars. 2 They use compasses, which point to north. 3 A lot of ships sank and pirates often attacked ships. 4 They use oil or diesel. 5 They use cruise ships. 6 They use bicycles.

Pages 40–41 **1** 1 high-speed train 2 steam train 3 articulated bus 4 tanker truck 5 bus 6 refrigerator truck **2** 1 150 2 300 3 9,288 4 160 5 200 **3** 1 steam trains 2 underground trains 3 diesel trains 4 high-speed trains **4** 1 coal 2 coal, water 3 water, steam 4 steam, engine 5 engine **5** 1 They built it in Wales in the United Kingdom. 2 A car uses the most fuel per passenger. 3 It takes six days to travel across Russia. 4 It was in London in the United Kingdom. 5 Because people travelled on buses to get to work as cities became bigger.

Pages 42–43 **1** 1 helmet 2 glove 3 brake 4 saddle 5 frame 6 tire 7 gears 8 back wheel 9 chain 10 pedal 11 front wheel **2** 1 light 2 small 3 comfortable 4 popular 5 thick, strong **3** 1 gears 2 bicycle 3 wood 4 faster **4** 1 true 2 true 3 true 4 true 5 false 6 false **5** 1 Because they had no tires. 2 They cycle to work or school, and for fun or sport. 3 A cyclist stops the bicycle with the brakes. 4 So that they can turn quickly.

Pages 44–45 **1** 1 steering wheel 2 engine 3 brake 4 seat belt 5 gears 6 front wheel 7 pedals 8 back wheel **2** 1 false 2 true 3 false 4 true 5 true 6 true 7 false 8 false **3** 1885: the first car; 1905 Rolls-Royce cars; 1913 Ford opened; 1927 15 million Model Ts were; 1950 were driving large cars; 1963 The Peel P50; 2005 was first made **4** 1 It had a gasoline engine and only three wheels. 2 Because they wanted to travel long distances. 3 A driver needs a key to start a car. 4 Seat belts and airbags protect them. 5 It helps the car to go faster because air can move easily over it.

Pages 46–47 **1** 1 tail 2 rudder 3 wing 4 engine 5 flap 6 cabin 7 wheel 8 nose 9 cockpit 10 pilot **2** 1 2003 2 90 3 2,140 4 1793 5 1903 6 850 **3** 1 airliner 2 balloon 3 rocket 4 airship 5 helicopter 6 plane 7 space shuttle **4** 1 Because a fire under the balloon heats the air inside the balloon. 2 There's a gas that is lighter than air. 3 The air under the wings pushes the plane up. 4 They sit in the cabin. 5 A person pedals it. 6 Because they can keep still in the air and they can fly in any direction. 7 free answers

Pages 48–49 **1** 1 cycle rickshaw 2 gondola 3 punt 4 snowmobile 5 auto rickshaw 6 sled **2** 1 sled 2 ox 3 cycle rickshaw 4 gondolier **3** 1 Khangai, Mongolia: carts, horses, camels 2 Delhi, India: buses, trains, bicycles, rickshaws 3 Oxford, United Kingdom: bicycles, punts 4 Nunavut, Canada: sleds, snowmobiles 5 Venice, Italy: boat, water buses, gondolas **4** 1 They travel by sled or snowmobile. 2 They use camels and horses. 3 Because there are no roads. 4 A punt is like a gondola. 5 A rickshaw has two wheels and a person pulls it, but a cycle rickshaw has three wheels and the driver pedals it. 6 They carry them in baskets or bicycle trailers.

Pages 50–51 **1** 1 plants 2 solar car 3 scramjet 4 transporter 5 jetpack 6 sails 7 maglev train 8 space plane **2** 1 no 2 no 3 yes 4 yes 5 no 6 yes **3** 1 true 2 true 3 false 4 false 5 true **4** 1 They will use sails to help power them. 2 We use plants. 3 We can get it from the sun and the wind. 4 Because it has an electric motor. 5 free answers

Subject Area

The World of Science & Technology

Topics & Curriculum Links

types of weather (Science)
weather, climates, and the environment (Geography)
changing climates (Geography; Science)
the water cycle (Science)
measurements, speeds, temperatures (Mathematics)
energy, fuel, and the environment (Science; Civics)
places and countries (Geography)
dates and events (History)

Vocabulary

weather; climates; seasons; places; transportation; energy; measurements; dates; numbers; countries; continents

Grammar

present simple; present continuous; past simple; present perfect; future simple; question forms; imperative; passive; adjectives; prepositions; adverbs

Teaching Ideas

See also pages 6–7 for general ideas that you can adapt. Or go to **www.oup.com/elt/teacher/readanddiscover**

Different Clouds

After reading Chapter 3, students look out for different clouds for a week. They can make notes about the types of cloud that they see, and what they look like. They can also take photos and write about what they see.

READ & TALK World Weather Research

After completing Project 2, students present their findings to the rest of the class. They can write and talk about their findings like this: *The weather was the same in ... It was different in ... [City] was the hottest / the coldest / had the most rain.* Students can also do further research into what the weather is like in the cities for a week, or a month, etc. Students then display all the weather information together. They can organize the information by continent or type of climate.

READ & TALK A Weather Debate

Students work in small groups. Give each group a type of weather, for example, hot, cold, dry, wet. Ask students to think of all the advantages of this type of weather, for example: *... weather is good because ... it's ... / you can ...* Then ask each group in turn to present their arguments, and any group can argue back with arguments against. Give a prize for the most convincing arguments.

Activities Answers

Pages 36–37 **1** 1 rain 2 cloud 3 sun 4 moon 5 stars 6 sky **2** 1 air 2 atmosphere 3 sun 4 mass 5 pushing 6 Low **3** 1 so that we can build the right type of homes. 2 so that they can travel at the right time. 3 so that they can plant and cut down crops at the right time. 4 so that they can avoid bad storms. **4** 1 A good way to predict the weather is to look at the clouds. 2 Today, scientists use computers to predict the weather. 3 In the past, people watched nature to predict the weather. 4 Some people think that if animals sit down, it will rain. 5 People believe that a red sky at night means good weather the next day.

Pages 38–39 **1** 1 cold climates 2 temperate climates 3 hot climates 4 equator **2** Hot Climate: free answers; Cold Climate: Antarctica and free answers; Temperate Climate: free answers **3** 1 climate 2 weather 3 climate 4 climate 5 weather 6 weather **4** 1 animals 2 coats 3 short 4 water 5 winter 6 summer 7 four 8 spring **5** 1 The climate is the usual weather for a place. 2 Land gets warm faster than the ocean. 3 Plains have the hottest weather. 4 Plains have hot summers and cold, dry winters.

Pages 40–41 **1** 1 Cirrus clouds are made of ice crystals. 2 Cumulus clouds are clouds that often bring good weather. 3 Stratus clouds are low, thin blankets of cloud. 4 Mist is very thin cloud. 5 Fog is thick cloud near the ground. **2** 1 A cloud can be as heavy as 100 elephants. 2 Clouds are made of millions of drops of water. 3 There are many different cloud shapes **3** 1 clouds 2 electricity 3 lightning 4 thunder 5 thunderstorm 6 tall **4** 1 Count the seconds between lightning and thunder. 2 Forked lightning and zigzag lightning. 3 About 100 times every year. 4 About 30,000 degrees centigrade. 5 free answers

Pages 42–43 **1** 1 red 2 orange 3 yellow 4 green 5 blue 6 indigo 7 violet **2** 1 overflow 2 deserts 3 animals 4 year 5 fertile 6 soil **3** 1 Rain falls into rivers and oceans. 2 The sun heats the water. 3 Some water changes into water vapor. 4 Water vapor rises into the sky. 5 Water vapor cools and changes back into water. 6 Drops of water fall from the clouds as rain. **4** 1 Two 2 For their crops to grow. 3 Destroy buildings and crops; kill animals and people (and make soil more fertile)

Pages 44–45 **1** 1 ice 2 hail 3 snow 4 sleet **2** 1 biggest hailstone ever recorded: 18 centimeters 2 parts of a snowflake: 6 3 the temperature when water freezes: 0°C 4 30% of Earth covered in ice: 11,000 years ago 5 some ice has been near the Poles: two million years 6 coldest temperature ever recorded: minus 89°C **3** 1 Rising air carries water drops up into the sky. 2 Water drops freeze and form hailstones. 3 Small hailstones start to fall. 4 Hailstones are pushed back up by the rising air. 5 Another layer of ice forms on the hailstones. 6 Hailstones become heavier than the air. 7 Heavy hailstones fall to the ground. **4** 1 freezes 2 snow 3 numb 4 sleet 5 hailstones 6 planes 7 whiteout 8 blizzard 9 avalanche. Secret word: South Pole **5** free answers

Pages 46–47 **1** 1 Weather is hottest in places near the equator. 2 Places with less than 25 centimeters of rain are called deserts. 3 Winds in the desert blow from the land to the ocean. 4 Nights in the desert can be very cold. 5 The Atacama Desert once had no rain for 400 years. **2** 1 true 2 true 3 false 4 true 5 false 6 true **3** 1 desert 2 sweat 3 sandstorm 4 hot 5 humid 6 fire 7 seed 8 drought 9 famine 10 dry **4** 1 Sandstorms can happen. 2 A few meters. 3 Three or more days. 4 Its humidity. 5 Because their sweat can't evaporate.

Pages 48–49 **1** 1 north-west 2 north 3 north-east 4 east 5 south-east 6 south 7 south-west 8 west **2** 1 light air = 3 kph 2 light breeze = 9 kph 3 gentle breeze = 15 kph 5 fresh breeze = 35 kph 6 strong breeze 45 kph 8 fresh gale = 68 kph 9 strong gale = 81 kph 11 storm = 110 kph 12 hurricane = 118 kph **3** 1 hurricane 2 tornado 3 tornado 4 hurricane 5 hurricane 6 tornado 7 tornado 8 hurricane 9 tornado 10 hurricane **4** 1 damage, things 2 cars, road 3 house, ground 4 building 5 Australia **5** free answers

Pages 50–51 **1** 1 warmer 2 faster 3 Earth 4 gas 5 heat 6 good **2** Why is the climate changing? power stations, heat, warm; What will happen in the future? Storms, droughts, famines, levels, go; What can we do? less, trees, walk, bicycle, energy **3** 1 climate 2 energy 3 solar energy 4 spring 5 rainbow 6 wind farm 7 blizzard 8 fog 9 warm 10 tornado **4** free answers

5 All About Islands

Subject Area

The Natural World

Topics & Curriculum Links

types of island (Geography)
how islands form (Geography)
places and countries (Geography)
oceans and continents (Geography)
plant and animal classification (Science)
parts of the body (Science)
dangers in the environment (Geography; Civics)
protecting plants and animals (Science; Civics)
tourism (Civics; Geography)
types of weather (Science)
weather and changing climates (Science; Geography; Civics)
man-made islands (Science; Technology;
dates and events (History)
quantities and measurements (Mathematics)

Vocabulary

places; forms of water; plants; animals; parts of the body; food; fruit; transportation; weather; seasons; buildings; numbers; measurements; countries; continents

Grammar

present simple; present continuous; past simple; future simple; present perfect; question forms; imperative; passive; adjectives; prepositions; adverbs

Teaching Ideas

See also pages 6–7 for general ideas that you can adapt. Or go to **www.oup.com/elt/teacher/readanddiscover**

READ & TALK An Island Presentation

After completing Project 2, students present their island to the rest of the class. They can describe the island, or other students can ask questions related to the topics on page 53 of the Reader, for example: *What is the island's name? What continent/ocean is it in? What amazing animals/interesting plants live there? How is the weather? What type of island is it? When did people arrive on the island?* Posters can then be displayed together, organizing them by type of island, or by continent.

READ & TALK An Island Quiz

Choose one of the islands from the Reader, and without saying its name, read out one fact about it and ask students to guess which island it is. Read out more facts, one at a time, until students guess the correct island. You can use a point scoring system, for example, five points after one fact, three points after two facts, etc. Students can then do this in small groups or pairs.

READ & TALK An Island Debate

Students work in small groups. Ask each group to choose an island that they would prefer to live on. Ask students to think of all the advantages of living on this island. Then ask each group in turn to present their arguments, and any group can argue back with arguments against. Give a prize for the most convincing argument!

Activities Answers

Page 36–37 **1** 1 North America 2 Australasia 3 Asia 4 South America 5 Antarctica 6 Europe 7 Africa **2** 1 false 2 true 3 true 4 true 5 false 6 false **3** 1 More than 70% of Earth's surface is water. 2 Less than 30 % of Earth's surface is land. 3 Sometimes waves move sand to form islands. 4 Volcanoes under the ocean can form new islands. 5 Some valleys and mountains can form new islands. 6 Solenodons live in Hispaniola. **4 Example answers** 1 An island is a piece of land with water all around it.2 There are thousands of islands. 3 free answers 5 free answers

Page 38–39 **1** 1 no 2 yes 3 yes 4 yes 5 yes 6 no 7 yes 8 yes 9 no 10 no **2** 1 from top to bottom – 5 6 1 4 3 2 **3** 1 300 2 2 3 1 4 17,500 5 6,000 **4** 1 Lava from a volcano under the ocean. 2 Some of the Canary Islands. 3 In warm volcanic ash. 4 Because the soil is fertile. 5 Rice and tropical fruit. 6 free answers

Page 40–41 **1** 1 sea turtle 2 coconut 3 jellyfish 4 coral 5 starfish 6 crab **2** 1 true 2 false 3 false 4 true 5 false 6 true **3** 1 animal 2 reefs 3 islands 4 jellyfish 5 bamboo 6 towers **4** 1 They push sand over a reef. 2 All the colors of the rainbow. 3 Because they are very poisonous. 4 With its legs. 5 On the island of Mauritius. 6 Because there weren't any other animals that hunted it.

Page 42–43 **1** 1 jumping spider 2 woolly rat 3 tree kangaroo 4 Galapagos tortoise 5 Komodo dragon 6 lemur **2** 1 lemur 2 tortoises 3 kangaroo 4 Komodo dragon 5 woolly rat 6 spider **3** 1 Indonesia 2 Madagascar 3 Pacific 4 Indian 5 New Guinea **4** 1 Because it's full of water. 2 To eat the leaves of trees. 3 The Komodo dragon. 4 To help it move in the trees and to communicate with other lemurs. 5 free answers

Page 44–45 **1** Pacific Ocean – Anuta, Atlantic Ocean Tristan da Cunha, Indian Ocean – Socotra, Pacific Ocean – Easter Island **2** 1 reptile 2 bird 3 reptile 4 fruit 5 fruit 6 bird 7 reptile 8 fruit **3** 1 cold, windy 2 fishermen 3 English 4 airport 5 telephones **4** 1 Because they are the families of the people who first came to the island. 2 It had big forests and a lot of birds. 3 They wanted the special red juice to use as a medicine. 4 It can change color. Its eyes can look in two different places at the same time.

Page 46–47 **1** 1 Greenland 2 New Guinea 3 Borneo 4 Madagascar 5 Baffin Island 6 Sumatra 7 Honshu 8 Britain **2** 1 false 2 true 3 true 4 false 5 true 6 false **3** 1 live 2 swim 3 fly 4 are 5 smell 6 eat **4** 1 So they can walk easily in the snow. 2 Seals 3 South Island, New Zealand 4 An insect – the heaviest insect on Earth. 5 It makes a horrible smell. 6 Wombat.

Page 48–49 **1** 1 Burma 2 rice 3 China 4 Japan 5 parks 6 Korea 7 reeds **2** 1 Odaiba Island is about 150 years old. 2 Intha men can row with their legs. 3 Burj Al Arab is one of the tallest hotels in the world 4 The Incheon bridge is more than 20 kilometers long. **3** 1 Sometimes people build cities on man-made islands. 2 The Intha people build houses on stilts. 3 There are hotels, stores, and homes on Palm Jumeirah. 4 Kansai was the first airport on a man-made island. 5 Five airports in Japan are on man-made islands. **4** 1 Because there isn't enough land. 2 Stores, restaurants, parks, and apartments. 3 The clear blue ocean. 4 321 meters. 5 free answers

Page 50–51 **1** 1 warmer 2 ice, higher 3 islands 4 kill 5 dies 6 tourists, life **2** 1 India, Bangladesh, Thailand, Norway 2 Maldive, Svalbard 3 Pacific, Indian, Arctic **3** 1 coral 2 protect 3 danger 4 seed 5 species 6 warm 7 levels 8 area 9 storms 10 ice 11 oil 12 land The secret word is conservation. **4** free answers

Subject Area

The Natural World

Topics & Curriculum Links

life cycles (Science)
animal classification (Science)
parts of the body (Science)
animals and their environments (Science; Geography)
dangers in the environment (Geography; Civics)
protecting animals (Science; Civics)
quantities and measurements (Mathematics)

Vocabulary

animals; parts of the body; places; food; weather; plants; measurements; numbers

Grammar

present simple; past simple; future simple; question forms; imperative; passive; adjectives; prepositions; adverbs

Teaching Ideas

See also pages 6–7 for general ideas that you can adapt. Or go to **www.oup.com/elt/teacher/readanddiscover**

READ & TALK A Life Cycle Presentation

After completing Project 1, students present their animal life cycle poster to the rest of the class. They can describe their animal and its life cycle, or other students can ask the questions on page 52 of the Reader. Posters can then be displayed together, organizing them by type of animal.

READ & TALK A Life Cycles Quiz

Ask the class true/false quiz questions, using facts from the Reader. Students can work in pairs or small groups. Then in pairs or small groups, students can ask their own questions.

Life Cycles Research

Students choose another animal and do research on its life cycle, using books or the Internet. They can choose an animal from their country, or an animal with a really amazing life cycle. Students then write about their findings and display the information. They can work in groups, and posters can then be displayed together, organizing them by type of animal, or habitat.

Activities Answers

Page 36–37 **1** 1 backbone 2 very small 3 arthropods 4 invertebrates 5 vertebrates **2** Invertebrates: Arthropods, snail, sponge, Flatworms, threadworm; Vertebrates: frog, Reptiles, Mammals **3** 1 animals that eat plants and animals: omnivores 2 when sperm joins with an egg: fertilization 3 animals that have a backbone: vertebrates 4 animals that produce sperm: males 5 animals that eat plants: herbivores 6 an important group of invertebrates: arthropods 7 an important group of vertebrates: reptiles 8 animals that eat other animals: carnivores 9 animals that produce eggs: females 10 animals that have no backbone: invertebrates **4 Example answers** 1 When animals are the same in many ways. 2 Because they hunt, cut down trees, and build houses and roads on land. 3 150 years 4 a few hours 5 No, they lay eggs. 6 They feed them milk, and some stay with them for many years.

Page 38–39 **1** 1 pupa 2 hatches 3 exoskeleton 4 larvae 5 cockroaches 6 molt 7 metamorphosis 8 nymphs 9 caterpillar 10 fireflies **2** 1 insect 2 an egg 3 incomplete 4 complete 5 30,000 **3** 1 a larva 2 a nymph 3 It comes off. 4 by singing 5 in a hole in dead wood 6 So that they are camouflaged.

Page 40–41 **1** Insects: bee, butterfly, cricket, locust; Other Invertebrates: spider, lobster, octopus, earthworm; Vertebrates: frog, hummingbird, gorilla, snake **2 Example answers** 1 They produce silk. 2 Most hatch after a few days or weeks. 3 Baby spiders are also called spiderlings; Another thing: free answers **3** 1 200,000 2 three 3 ten 4 12 5 10,000, ten 6 25 **4** 1 Lobsters live at the top of the ocean after they hatch. 2 Earthworms are hermaphrodites. 3 Octopuses put their eggs in strings. 4 Lobsters carry their eggs hidden under their tail. 5 Earthworms have male and female parts. 6 Octopuses die after their eggs hatch. 7 Lobsters often eat their old shell after molting. 8 Earthworms keep their eggs in special rings. 9 Octopuses live in dens at the bottom of the ocean.

Page 42–43 **1** Fish: water, cold-blooded; Young Fish: no fins, can't swim well, predators (seals, birds, frogs, and other fish), Food: yolk bag, small plants, insect eggs or larvae **2** 1 seahorse 2 shark 3 tuna fish 4 whale shark 5 stickleback 6 salmon **3** 1 true 2 false 3 true 4 true 5 false 6 false **4** 1 hatch 2 swim 3 breed 4 die; (picture order, left to right): 2, 1, 4, 3

Page 44–45 **1** Amphibian Larvae: (✗), (✓), (✓), (✗); Amphibian Adults: (✓), (✗), (✗), (✓); 1 Amphibian larvae don't have lungs. They have gills. 2 Amphibian adults have lungs and usually live on land. **2** 1 salamander 2 midwife toad 3 tadpole 4 darwin's frog **3** 1 Most amphibians live for some of their life in ~~air~~ water and for some of their life on land. 2 Only ~~50%~~ 5% of the eggs that frogs lay will become adults. 3 During metamorphosis, many amphibians become ~~herbivores~~ carnivores. 4 Most amphibians go to ~~dry~~ wet places to breed. **4** 1 thousands 2 They close. 3 Through their skin and their lungs. 4 Because they can only breathe through their skin if it's wet. 5 They croak and shout.

Page 46–47 **1** 1 turtle 2 lizard 3 snake 4 crocodile **2** 1 If a predator catches a lizard, the lizard can break off its tail. 2 Monitor lizards fight for a mate. 3 To find a mate, crocodiles blow bubbles in the water. 4 When a snake grows, its old skin come off. 5 Alligators make a nest from mud and leaves. **3** 1 cold-blooded 2 scales 3 legs 4 whiptail **4** 1 true 2 true 3 false 4 true **5** 1 Most reptiles hatch from eggs. 2 Chameleons can change color. 3 Alligators lay their eggs in a big nest. 4 Snakes find their mate by smell.

Page 48–49 **1** (top to bottom, left to right): (✓), (✗), (✓), (✓), (✓), (✗); 1 Birds have feathers. 2 Birds don't have fur or hair. 3 Birds lay eggs. 4 Birds have wings. 5 Birds built nests. 6 Birds don't feed their babies milk. **2** 1 It's when male birds try to find female birds that they can mate with. 2 To keep their eggs and chicks safe and warm. 3 Usually brown and speckled. 4 To fly to warmer places for winter. **3** 1 frigate bird: he pushes his red throat out 2 blue-footed booby: he shows his big blue feet 3 songbird: he sings 4 bower bird: he builds a special place with bright colored things inside **4 Example answers** 1 grass, mud, twigs 2 trees, cliffs, ground 3 to fly, to feed, to sing, to keep safe **5** 1 Birds keep their eggs warm. 2 Ostriches lay the biggest eggs. 3 Chicks have a special 'tooth' on their beak. 4 Cuckoos lay their eggs in other birds' nests.

Page 50–51 **1** 1 polar bear 2 anteater 3 giraffe 4 person 5 leopard 6 kangaroo 7 shrew 8 elephant; (in correct order) 1 It digs a den in the snow so its babies will be warm. (polar bear) 2 It carries its babies on its back for the first year. (anteater) 3 It fights with its neck with other males when it's ready to mate. (giraffe) 4 You are one! (person) 5 It makes marks on trees when it's looking for a mate. (leopard) 6 It grows in its mother's pouch for up to a year after it is born. (kangaroo) 7 Its gestation time is only two weeks. (shrew) 8 It stays close to its mother until it's ten years old. (elephant) **2** 1 2 2 5 3 females 4 milk 5 fur or hair **3** 1 gestation 2 placenta 3 marsupials 4 habitats **4** Insects: butterfly (and free answers)

5 Exploring Our World

Subject Area

The Natural World

Topics & Curriculum Links

explorers and exploring (Geography; History)
places and countries (Geography)
plants and animals (Science)
natural resources (Science)
physical processes (Geography)
transportation (Technology)
directions and orientation (Geography; Technology)
sizes and measurements (Mathematics)
dates and events (History)

Vocabulary

explorers; places; transportation; plants; animals; materials; measurements; dates; numbers; countries; nationalities; continents

Grammar

present simple; present continuous; past simple; present perfect; past continuous; future simple; question forms; imperative; passive; adjectives; prepositions; adverbs

Teaching Ideas

See also pages 6–7 for general ideas that you can adapt. Or go to **www.oup.com/elt/teacher/readanddiscover**

READ & TALK Exploring Research

After completing Project 1, students choose another explorer and do research using books or the Internet, to find out where, when, what, and how they explored. They can choose a famous explorer from their country, or an explorer who explored their country. Students then write about their findings and display the information. They can use a copy of the world map from page 7 to show where the explorer went.

READ & TALK An Exploring Quiz

Ask the class quiz questions, using facts from the Reader. Students can work in pairs or small groups. Then in pairs or small groups, students can ask their own questions, for example: *Who ...? When did ...? Where did ...?*

READ & TALK An Exploring Debate

Students work in small groups. Ask each group where they would like to explore, why, what they would do there, etc. Then in turn each group presents their arguments for the place that they have chosen. Give a prize for the most convincing arguments.

Activities Answers

Pages 36–37 **1** 1 mountain 2 map 3 river 4 compass 5 forest 6 satellite **2** 1 true 2 true 3 false 4 true 5 false 6 true 7 false 8 true **3** 1 Early explorers wanted to find new places. 2 They explored deserts, rivers, and mountains. 3 They crossed land and explored oceans. 4 Explorers want to go somewhere a new way. 5 Some explorers look for new ways to travel. 6 Others want to be the fastest to do something. **4** 1 stars 2 maps 3 mountains, rivers 4 compass 5 north 6 instruments

Pages 38–39 **1** 1 North America 2 Pacific Ocean 3 Atlantic Ocean 4 Europe 5 Africa 6 South America 7 Asia 8 Indian Ocean 9 Antarctica **2** 1 Early people traveled around to look for ~~rocks~~ food. 2 Zhang Qian was an early explorer from ~~Europe~~ China. 3 Marco Polo traveled from ~~Africa~~ Europe to China. 4 Ibn Battuta explored ~~North America~~ North Africa, the Middle East, and Asia. **3** 1 In 1405, Zheng He traveled from China to East Africa. 2 In 1488, Bartolomeu Dias traveled from Europe to Africa. 3 In 1492, Christopher Columbus traveled from Europe to America. 4 In 1498, Vasco da Gama traveled from Europe to India. 5 In 1520, Ferdinand Magellan traveled from Europe to Asia. 6 In 1642, Abel Tasman traveled to New Zealand. 7 In 1773, James Cook traveled to the Antarctic. 8 In 1895, Henryk Bull traveled from Europe to Africa. **4** free answers

Pages 40–41 **1** 1 understand 2 rocks 3 plates 4 an earthquake 5 fossils 6 animals **2** 1 explore the past 2 make a mountain 3 earthquakes will happen 4 on Mount Everest 5 under the ocean **3** geologists, rocks, made; paleontologists, fossils, animals; archaeologists, wore **4** 1 It helped them to understand the Ancient Egyptian alphabet. 2 in Egypt 3 About how the Mayan and Aztec people lived. 4 4,500 years old 5 cave paintings 6 in the Andes

Pages 42–43 **1** 1 30% 2 less 3 bigger 4 four 5 sandy 6 dry 7 hot **2** 1 People have explored deserts for many years. 2 Some early desert explorers went to find new trade routes. 3 Some explorers want to learn about the people who live in deserts. 4 Some explorers want an adventure. 5 There can be salt, oil, or gold under deserts. 6 Archaeologists have found villages buried under the sand. 7 An American explorer found dinosaur bones in the Gobi Desert **3** 1 Many early desert explorers went to find ~~deserts~~ things to trade. 2 René Caillé traveled across the Sahara Desert ~~by train~~ with camels. 3 Camels can walk a long way without food or ~~clothes~~ water. 4 Francis Younghusband crossed the ~~Australian~~ Gobi Desert. 5 Robyn Davidson crossed the ~~Sahara~~ Australian Desert in 1977. **4** Good things: new, famous; Bad things; lost, hot **5** free answers

Pages 44–45 **1** 1 true 2 false 3 true 4 true **2** 1 land 2 plants 3 flowers 4 rainforest 5 discover 6 climb **3** 1 spices 2 sugar 3 chocolate 4 coffee 5 chewing gum 6 rubber 7 medicines 8 fruit 9 nuts **4** 1 New types of plant or animal. 2 The Missouri River, in America. 3 Many new types of fish. 4 14,712 types of insect.

Pages 46–47 **1** 1 Antarctic 2 see 3 minerals 4 ends 5 quickly, vehicles **2** 1 Antarctic 2 Antarctic 3 Arctic 4 Antarctic 5 Arctic 6 Antarctic 7 Arctic 8 Antarctic **3** 1 In 1500, European explorers reached the Arctic. 2 In 1728, Vitus Bering sailed into the Northeast Passage. 3 In 1906, Roald Amundsen found the Northwest Passage. 4 In 1909, Robert Peary reached the North Pole. 5 In 1911, Roald Amundsen reached the South Pole. 6 In 1958, Vivian Fuchs crossed Antarctica. 7 In 2001, Ann Bancroft and Liv Arnesen were the first women to cross Antarctica. **4** free answers

Pages 48–49 **1** 1 Mountains are ~~lower~~ higher than the land around them. 2 Mountains cover about ~~50%~~ 25% of Earth. 3 The ~~smallest~~ biggest mountain chain is the Himalayas. 4 Mount Everest is growing about 5 millimeters every ~~week~~ year. 5 The Mid-Atlantic Ridge is under the ~~Pacific~~ Atlantic Ocean. 6 The ~~tallest~~ longest mountain chain on land is the Andes. **2** **Example answers** 1 To learn more about how Earth was made. 2 To look for ancient remains. 3 To be the first to climb a mountain. 4 To win a prize. **3** 1 stones 2 medicines 3 first 4 people 5 highest **4** 1492: Mont Aiguille; 1786: Gabriel Paccard, Mont Blanc; 1953: Edmund Hillary; 1975: Everest; 1999: volcano; 2003: Ming Kipa Sherpa

Pages 50–51 **1** 1 enormous 2 five 3 half 4 flat 5 plains 6 higher **2** 1 oil 2 salt 3 Pearls 4 fish 5 iron 6 seaweed **3** 1 Oceans are full of amazing plants and animals. 2 Scientists find more than 100 new types of fish every year. 3 Early ocean explorers could only explore for as long as they could breathe. 4 In 1960, two explorers dived to the deepest part of the Pacific Ocean. **4** 1 a small submarine 2 some new types of fish 3 more than 7,000 hours 4 Because they can send robots to explore places. **5** free answers

Subject Area

The World of Science & Technology

Topics & Curriculum Links

migrating animals (Science)
types of migration (Science)
animal life cycles (Science)
dangers in the environment (Geography; Civics)
changing climates (Geography; Science)
protecting animals (Science; Civics)
places and countries (Geography)
sizes and measurements (Mathematics)

Vocabulary

animals; parts of the body; places; weather; climate; seasons; plants; buildings; measurements; numbers; countries; continents

Grammar

present simple; present continuous; past simple; present perfect; future simple; question forms; imperative; passive; adjectives; prepositions; adverbs

Teaching Ideas

See also pages 6–7 for general ideas that you can adapt. Or go to **www.oup.com/elt/teacher/readanddiscover**

READ & TALK An Animal Presentation

After completing Project 1, students present one of their animals to the rest of the class. They can talk or write about it like this: *It's a / an ... It's ... It migrates ... kilometers from ... to ...* Or students can talk about their animal without saying its name, and ask the class to guess the animal. This could also be done in pairs. Posters can then be displayed together. Students can also use a copy of the world map on page 7 to show the different migration routes.

READ & TALK A Migrations Survey

After completing Project 2, students collect the survey information from the class. They can do this by listening to each student giving their information in turn, or by collecting the information in a big chart on the board. Then they make a poster to show the class results.

READ & TALK A Migrations Quiz

Ask the class quiz questions, using facts from the Reader, or describe an animal from the Reader. Students can work in pairs or small groups to answer the questions or to guess the animal. Then in pairs or small groups, students can do their own quiz.

Activities Answers

Pages 36–37 **1** **1** food, water, live, breed **2** longer, shorter, hotter, colder, food, chemicals **3** landmarks, sun, moon, stars, smells, sounds, Earth's magnetic field **4** bad weather, predators **2** **1** migration: when animals move from one place to another **2** migrant: an animal that migrates **3** complete migration: when all the animals in a species migrate **4** partial migration: when only some animals in a species migrate **5** predators: animals that kill and eat other animals **3** **1** ~~breed~~ migrate **2** ~~week~~ year **3** ~~garden~~ field **4** ~~Zebras~~ Bats **5** ~~smells~~ echoes

Pages 38–39 **1** **1** New Zealand **2** China **3** Alaska **4** Florida **5** Wisconsin **2** **1** south, north **2** north, south **3** east, west **4** Tropics **3** **1** Bar-tailed godwits fly further without stopping than any other bird. **2** Bar-tailed godwits fly 11,500 kilometers without stopping. **3** Geese and cranes learn where to go from their parents. **4** Geese and cranes fly in a V-shape. **5** Whooping cranes almost became extinct in the USA. **6** Whooping cranes have learned to migrate by following planes. **4** **1** Because it's too cold and there is not enough food. **2** Because days are long, and they can find food for their young. **3** They eat a lot of food, double their weight, muscles become stronger, they molt. **4** Good weather. **5** Hunters, tall buildings, loss of habitats from farming or building.

Pages 40–41 **1** **1** larvae **2** old skin **3** habitats **4** south **5** trees **6** eggs **2** **1** fall **2** less **3** millions **4** body **5** winter **3** **1** larvae: baby animals that change when they become adults **2** irruptive migration: when animals move away because there are too many in one place **3** wet season: the rainy time in the Tropics **4** swarms: large groups of insects **4** **1** Because they live for less than a year. **2** They change color, and they change how they live. **3** More than 1,000 kilometers. **4** During the wet season.

Pages 42–43 **1** **1** Reindeer migrate in big herds to find grass and lichens. **2** Lemmings migrate to new places when there are too many of them. **3** Frogs and toads migrate to water to breed. **2** **1** deer, Arctic **2** north, grass **3** snow, lichens **4** grow **3** **1** Because they live in large groups. **2** Because there are fewer predators. **3** Because there is too much snow and not enough food. **4** To find a new place to live with lots of food. **4** **1** tunnels **2** lemmings **3** lichens **4** toad **5** chamois **6** Sami **7** herd **8** wolves

Pages 44–45 **1** **1** one **2** 3,000 **3** 200,000, 500,000 **4** 100, 300 **5** 80 **6** six **2** **1** giraffe **2** zebra **3** hyena **4** gazelle **5** lion **6** buffalo **7** crane **8** leopard **3** **1** eat **2** migrate **3** fight **4** thin **4** **1** rain **2** north, south **3** Serengeti **4** rivers **5** grass **6** Male **7** find a mate **8** grass

Pages 46–47 **1** **1** humpback whale. Favorite food: krill; Lives (summer): polar oceans; Lives (winter): warmer, tropical oceans; Amazing facts: migrates further than any other mammal, makes special sounds **2** **1** squid **2** dolphin **3** penguin **4** tuna **5** plankton **6** sea turtle **3** **1** mothers **2** male **3** 16 **4** feed **5** vertical **4** **1** tuna **2** penguin **3** humpback **4** plankton **5** krill **6** shark **5** **1** Up to 17,000 kilometers every year. **2** To breed. **3** To find krill. **4** So that ocean currents will carry the eggs away from predators. **5** To eat plant plankton.

Pages 48–49 **1** **1** hatch **2** migrate **3** ocean **4** adult **5** breed **6** larvae **7** young **8** rivers **9** ocean **2** **1** Salmon migrate from the ocean to rivers to breed. **2** Bears hunt salmon when they swim up rivers. **3** Eels migrate from rivers to the ocean to breed. **4** Sea turtles lay their eggs on land **3** **1** land **2** ocean **3** sand **4** ocean **4** **1** They use smell. **2** They change color from silver to red. **3** Fish ladders. **4** Their stomachs become smaller and their eyes become much bigger.

Pages 50–51 **1** **1** fishing, hunting **2** roads, power lines, wind turbines **3** trees, ponds, dams, fences **4** storms, ice on polar oceans, deserts, ocean currents **2** **1** albatrosses **2** willow warbler **3** Polar bears **4** seals **5** Cod **3** **1** Because our vehicles, factories, and power stations are making too many gases like carbon dioxide. **2** Because the climate is changing. **3** On the ice in the Arctic. **4** There is less ice to walk on so they have to swim too far. **5** To help them see where the animals are migrating.

5 Homes Around the World

Subject Area

The World of Arts & Social Studies

Topics & Curriculum Links

building materials (Science; Technology)
homes and climates (Geography)
sizes and measurements (Mathematics)
shapes (Technology; Mathematics)
energy and the environment (Science; Civics)
poverty and being homeless (Civics)
countries (Geography)
dates and events (History)

Vocabulary

homes; rooms; materials; shapes; weather; climates; places; transportation; measurements; dates; numbers; countries; nationalities; continents

Grammar

present simple; present continuous; past simple; future simple; question forms; imperative; passive; adjectives; prepositions; adverbs

Teaching Ideas

See also pages 6–7 for general ideas that you can adapt. Or go to **www.oup.com/elt/teacher/readanddiscover**

Famous Homes Research

After reading Chapter 5, students do research, using books or the Internet, about another famous home. They can write about their findings and display the information, using the models in Chapter 5 for guidance. Students can work in groups, and posters can then be displayed together.

READ & TALK An Unusual Home Design

After completing Project 2, students present their unusual home design to the rest of the class. They can write and talk about it like this: *My home is made of ... It has ... The ... is used for ... It's unusual because ...* They then display all the designs together, and students write comments on each other's design. Then they can vote for their favorite design.

Homes Research

Students choose a type of material that is used to build homes or things inside homes, for example, wood, glass, stone. Or they can choose a part of the world, or a particular climate, and find out about homes built there. They do research using books or the Internet, and then write about their findings and display the information. Students can work in groups, and posters can then be displayed together.

READ & TALK A Homes Debate

Students work in groups. Give each group a type of home, for example, house, cave, apartment, houseboat, igloo, castle. Ask students to think of all the advantages of living in this type of home, like this: *It's good to live in a ... because it's / you can ...* Then ask each group in turn to present their arguments, and any group can argue back with arguments against. Give a prize for the most convincing argument!

Activities Answers

Pages 36–37 **1** 1 stone house 2 mud house 3 wooden house 4 castle 5 cave 6 straw house **2** 1 50,000; 2 5,000; 3 3,400; 4 2,400; 5 2,000; **3** 1 false 2 true 3 true 4 false 5 false 6 false **4** e, d, f, a, b, c 1 Mix mud and straw. 2 Put the mixture into molds. 3 Leave the molds in the sun. 4 Build a wall. 5 Leave holes for windows and doors. 6 Put wet mud on the wall.

Pages 38–39 **1** 1 cottage (Country) 2 terraced houses (City) 3 skyscraper (City) 4 bungalow (City and Country) 5 detached house (Country) **2** 1 false 2 true 3 false 4 true 5 false 6 false 7 true 8 false **3 example answers** 1 Houses in a row are called *terraced.* 2 Tall buildings in cities are called *skyscrapers.* 3 Rich people sometimes live in mansions. 4 Houses in the country often have gardens. 5 *Detached* houses have space all around them. **4** free answers

Pages 40–41 **1** 1 polar 2 mountainous 3 tropical 4 desert 5 temperate **2** free answer **3** Polar: cold, windy, snowy, icy; Tropical: hot, wet, sunny; Desert: hot, cold, windy, sunny, dry; Temperate: mild, sunny **4** 1 hot 2 snow 3 mild 4 stone 5 cold 6 wet 7 floods 8 underground 9 **example answer** A *chalet* has a long sloping roof. 10 **example answer** Houses in tropical climates are often built on *stilts.*

Pages 42–43 **1** 1 boat 2 wagon 3 tent 4 wagon 5 tent 6 wagon 7 boat **2** 1 tent 2 motor home 3 houseboat 4 wagon **3** 1 Teepees are made from animal skins. 2 Some houseboats are floating shops. 3 Canal boats are long and thin. 4 Wagons were pulled by oxen. 5 Many people like to go camping. 6 The Uros people make floating houses. **4** 1 Because their animals need fresh grass to eat. 2 So that they can travel along narrow rivers or canals. 3 They are pulled by horses. 4 They sleep in tents and cook their food outside.

Pages 44–45 **1** 1 The White House 2 Topkapi Palace 3 Windsor Castle 4 The Forbidden City **2** 1 The Queen of the United Kingdom has two homes. 2 In November 1992 there was a fire at Windsor Castle. 3 The White House is in the USA. 4 43 presidents have lived in the White House. 5 The Forbidden City is in Beijing. 6 The Forbidden City took 15 years to build. **3** Buckingham Palace: gardens, art gallery, flag; The White House: gardens, movie theater, flag, swimming pool; Topkapi Palace: gardens, museum; The Forbidden City: high walls, gardens, museum, moat **example answer** 1 The Forbidden City has high walls. 2 Buckingham Palace, the White House, Topkapi Palace and the Forbidden City have gardens. 3 Topkapi Palace and the Forbidden City have museums. 4 Buckingham Palace has an art gallery. 5 The Forbidden City has a moat. 6 The White House has a movie theater. 7 Buckingham Palace and the White House have flags. 8 The White House has a swimming pool.

Pages 46–47 **1** Natural: mud, wood, stone; Man-Made: concrete, glass, bottles, cans, plastic, bricks **2** 1 Cave homes today are very comfortable. 2 The cave homes in Guadix have chimneys to let air in. 3 Cave homes today do have Internet connections. 4 The Toraja houses have roofs shaped like boats. 5 Architects sometimes copy things from nature. **3** 1 chimneys, windows, water, electricity (also television and Internet) 2 car tires, cans, plastic bottles, mud 3 Antonio Gaudi, Frank Lloyd Wright 4 Spain, USA, El Salvador, Japan (also Indonesia) **4** free answer

Pages 48–49 **1** 1 orphanage 2 old people's home 3 refugee camp 4 *tulou* **2** 1 Some old people live near their families. 2 A *tulou* is made of mud. 3 A *yano* doesn't have any walls. 4 Children with no parents are called orphans. 5 Some people's homes are destroyed by floods. 6 About 12 million people live in refugee camps. **3** 1 2 or 3; 2 800; 3 400; 4 3 or 4; 5 1; 6 0; **4** 1 In a refugee camp. 2 They can talk, play games, and keep each other company. 3 They can look after the children while the parents work. 4 It's made from leaves. 5 They sleep in hammocks. 6 It's a big home where children with no parents live.

Pages 50–51 **1** 1 friendly 2 sun 3 television 4 fridge 5 waterproof 6 concrete 7 energy 8 damages 9 space 10 wind 11 computer; the secret word is: environment **2** 1 float 2 bad 3 wind 4 warm 5 Brick 6 cheap **3** free answer

Subject Area

The World of Arts & Social Studies

Topics & Curriculum Links

types of art (Art)
colors, shapes, and perspective (Art; Technology)
urban and rural landscapes (Art; Geography; Civics)
materials (Science; Technology)
famous artists (Art, History)
plants and animals (Science)
tools and machines (Technology)
types of light (Science, Art)
people and daily life (History; Civics)
places and countries (Geography)
dates and events (History)
quantities and measurements (Mathematics)

Vocabulary

types of art; materials; shapes; buildings; weather; animals; plants; fruit; parts of the body; clothes; sports; transportation; furniture; numbers; measurements; places; countries; continents

Grammar

present simple; present continuous; past simple; future simple; present perfect; question forms; imperative; passive; adjectives; prepositions; adverbs

Teaching Ideas

See also pages 6–7 for general ideas that you can adapt. Or go to **www.oup.com/elt/teacher/readanddiscover**

READ & TALK My Favorite Picture

After completing Project 2, students present their favorite artist to the rest of the class. Students then display all the pictures together, organizing them by type of art, or artist's nationality. Then they can vote for their favorite picture.

READ & TALK Which Picture Is It?

Choose a picture from the Reader, and ask students to guess which picture it is. Describe it to the class without saying which page it's on, for example: *It's a [type of art]. There's a ... It's ... It has ...* Then ask students to do the same in pairs, taking turns to describe a picture.

Art Research

Using books or the Internet, students do research on famous artists who live/lived and/or work/worked in their country. They can write about them like this: *[Name] lives/lived in ... and paints/painted/draws/drew/makes/made ...; He/She is famous because he/she ...* They can also add pictures of the artists and their art, and the work can be displayed as a class mural.

Activities Answers

Page 36–37 **1** **1** countryside **2** sky **3** bridge **4** window **5** snow **6** dome **2** **1** city **2** Spain **3** people **4** painting **5** artist **6** perspective **3** **1** Gustave Caillebotte painted some people in Paris. **2** The people are on a bridge **3** There is a man and a woman. **4** They are talking. **5** Another man is watching something. **6** The artist used perspective in this picture. **4** **1** El Greco painted Toledo in about 1600. **2** They are on a bridge in Paris. **3** A dog. **4** The season is winter.

Page 38–39 **1** **1** interior **2** room **3** China **4** artist **5** perspective **6** vanishing **2** **1** China **2** was **3** two **4** people **5** talking **6** man **7** really **3** **1** Look carefully at the painting on page 10. **2** It's a painting of a room in Cairo. **3** There are interesting things in this painting. **4** Three cats are sleeping on the floor. **5** Outside I is warm and sunny. **6** Sunlight is coming through the door. **4** **1** two people. **2** a boy. **3** some bread. **4** perspective. **5** far away. **6** Pieter de Hooch.

Page 40–41 **1** **1** A landscape is a painting of the countryside. **2** In some landscapes there aren't any people. **3** The countryside is the most important thing. **4** Some landscapes are of mountains. **5** Sunlight on mountains can look amazing. **6** Do you like paintings of mountains? **2** **1** amazing **2** landscape **3** Chinese **4** countryside **5** map **3** **1** He was from Mexico **2** The mountains. **4** A rich man with his friends. **4** **1** Mexico **2** born **3** countryside **4** beautiful **5** **1** Ando Hiroshige was from Japan. **2** He was born in 1797. **3** He painted the countryside in Japan. **4** He painted beautiful landscapes.

Page 42–43 **1** **1** flowers **2** paintbrush **3** bowl **4** melon **5** butterfly **6** guitar **2** **1** In a still life, there are often people flowers or food. **2** In the still life on page 17, there's a big piece of apple melon. **3** This still life is by an artist from France Germany. **4** The artist was a man woman. **5** His Her painting has big, strong shapes. **3** **1** Jan Van Kessel was from Europe. **2** He painted a still life with flowers. **3** It's a beautiful painting. **4** Grinling Gibbons was born in 1648. **5** He made sculptures for big houses. **6** His family still makes things with wood. **4** **1** Adjectives – amazing, beautiful, easy, funny Types of Painting – landscape, interior, still life, portrait Things in Still Life – food, fruit, musical instruments, flowers

Page 44–45 **1** **1** robot **2** factory **3** mural **4** building site **5** notebook **6** helicopter **2** **1** Seven. **2** They are in a car factory. **3** They are working with machines. **4** Diego Rivera. **3** **1** Grygoriy Shyshko is from Ukraine. **2** He painted a building site. **3** There are big machines in his painting. **4** We can also see a man. **5** He works with the machines. **6** Is this a beautiful painting? **4** **1** Mexico **2** factory **3** machines **5** famous **5** **1** Leonardo da Vinci was born in Florence. **2** He drew ideas for flying machines in about 1490. **3** He was interested in everything. **4** He was an amazing man.

Page 46–47 **1** **1** sun **2** moon **3** shade **4** ink **5** candle **6** dots **2** **1** Italy **2** was **3** Japanese **4** gray **5** France **6** sitting **3** **1** brighter **2** gray **3** bright **4** shade **5** candlelight **6** dots **4** **1** It's a hot, sunny day. **2** Seven, and some in a boat on the river. **3** They are at the river near Paris. **4** They are sitting by the river or standing in the river. Some people are in a boat. **5** A dog.

Page 48–49 **1** **1** Henri Rousseau was a French artist. **2** He painted some soccer players. **3** They are wearing funny clothes. **4** Ida Schwetz-Lehmann was an Austrian artist. **5** She made some small sculptures of women. **6** The women are holding their hats. **2** **1** In the painting on page 28, the people are ~~swimming~~ dancing. **2** They are moving ~~slowly~~ fast. **3** We can can't see them very well. **3** **1** The painting on page 28 shows some dancers. **2** Maybe they are at a party. **3** An Austrian artist made the sculptures on page 30. **4** They are sculptures of women in the wind. **5** On page 30 there is a painting of a storm. **4** **1** There are four. **2** They are wearing striped clothes. **3** Ivan Aivazovsky painted it. **4** A car moving fast. **5** The artist uses lines.

Page 50–51 **1** **1** park **2** full **3** boats **4** blocks **5** artists **6** installations **2** **1** It's in Saudi Arabia. **2** Richard Stringer. **3** He was 89 years old. **4** They wrapped a building. **3** **1** bird **2** red **3** people **4** idea **5** Melbourne **4** **1** page 30 **2** page 33 **3** page 27 **4** page 22 **5** page 12 **6** page 20 **5** free answers

Subject Area

The World of Science & Technology

Topics & Curriculum Links

types of cells and microbes (Science)
inside animal cells and plant cells (Science)
how cells work; respiration and diffusion (Science)
how cells fight infections; keeping clean (Science; Civics)
cell reproduction (Science)
food and healthy eating (Science; Civics)
plants and animals (Science)
parts of the body (Science)
photosynthesis (Science)
dates and events (History)

Vocabulary

animals; parts of the body; plant parts; food; fuel; places; dates; numbers; measurements

Grammar

present simple; past simple; past continuous; past perfect; question forms; imperative; passive; adjectives; prepositions; adverbs

Teaching Ideas

See also pages 6–7 for general ideas that you can adapt. Or go to **www.oup.com/elt/teacher/readanddiscover**

READ & TALK A New Microbe Presentation

After completing Project 1, students present their new microbe to the rest of the class. Posters can then be displayed together, and students vote for the most convincing new microbe.

READ & TALK A Cells Quiz

Ask the class quiz questions, using facts from the Reader. Ask true/false questions, or questions starting with *What, Where, When,* etc., or give a definition and ask students to provide the answer. Students can work in pairs or small groups. Then in pairs or small groups, students can ask their own questions.

A Photosynthesis Experiment

Ask students to grow three small plants at home, with the help of an adult. They grow each plant in a different condition: 1 light and water; 2 light only; 3 water only. Students record their findings every day for a few weeks.

Activities Answers

Page 36–37 **1** 1 microscope 2 cell 3 microbe 4 tissue 5 organ 6 scientist **2** 1 smallest 2 microscope 3 million 4 cell 5 amoeba **3** 1 tissues 2 bark 3 eye 4 roots **4** 1 There are different types of cell in plant and animal bodies. 2 Tissues are the same cells that work together. 3 Cells that work together do the same job. 4 Different tissues that work together make an organ. **5 Example answers** 1 Because they look like little rooms called cells. 2 They can get energy from food, move, grow, and reproduce. 3 free answers

Page 38–39 **1** 1 cytoplasm 2 nucleus 3 cell membrane **2** 1 The cell membrane holds the cells together. 2 The nucleus controls what happens inside the cell. 3 The cytoplasm is where chemical reactions happen. **3** 1 different 2 oxygen 3 round 4 vessels 5 five **4** 1 The cell membrane lets substances move inside and out of the cell. 2 Some chemical reactions in the cytoplasm make new substances for the cell. 3 Inside the nucleus there's a chemical code called DNA. 4 DNA controls how the cell grows, moves, and reproduces. **5 Example answers** 1 all around an animal's body 2 They have long fibers. 3 by using their fibers 4 They help us to stay safe.

Page 40–41 **1** 1 cell wall 2 cell membrane 3 vacuole 4 chloroplast 5 nucleus 6 cytoplasm **2** 1 false 2 true 3 true 4 false 5 true **3** 1 nucleus 2 outside 3 cellulose 4 shape 5 strongest 6 paper **4** 1 Chloroplasts give leaves and stems their green color. 2 Chloroplasts catch and store energy from sunlight. 3 Plants take in water through their roots. 4 Leaves take in carbon dioxide through holes called stomata. 5 Plant cells use carbon dioxide and water to make food. 6 Sugar is a type of food for the plant.

Page 42–43 **1** 1 diatom 2 amoeba 3 bacteria 4 slime mold **2** 1 There are ~~a few~~ many different types of microbe. 2 Microbes live in ~~a few~~ many different places. 3 An amoeba is ~~bigger~~ smaller than a grain of salt. 4 Amoebas eat microbes that are ~~bigger~~ smaller than they are. 5 An amoeba ~~quickly~~ slowly digests its food. **3** 1 The cell wall of a diatom looks like thin glass. 2 Bacteria were some of the first living things on Earth. 3 Some bacteria eat the food between people's teeth. 4 Some bacteria survive where other living things can't. **4** 1 By making their body into a circle shape around the food. 2 They use sunlight to make food by photosynthesis. 3 almost anything 4 They join together in a group. 5 Because they make half of all the oxygen in the air.

Page 44–45 **1** 1 mitochondria 2 oxygen 3 respiration 4 energy 5 breathing 6 diffusion 7 waste 8 cells 9 lungs 10 blood **2** 1 inside 2 food 3 oxygen 4 a lot of **3** 1 What part of a cell controls what goes in and out? The cell membrane controls what goes in and out. 2 What do all chemical reactions in a cell make? All chemical reactions make waste. 3 What type of waste do cells make during respiration? They make carbon dioxide waste. 4 What does the cell membrane do with waste? It lets it leave the cell. **4** 1 diffusion 2 more, less 3 Oxygen 4 Carbon dioxide

Page 46–47 **1** 1 false 2 true 3 true 4 false 5 false 6 false **2** 1 two 2 smaller 3 grow 4 divide 5 the same as **3** 1 reproduce 2 eggs 3 identical 4 sperm 5 DNA 6 cell 7 complete 8 children **4** 1 by dividing in half 2 new skin tissue 3 So that plants and animals can grow, or to replace old or dead cells.

Page 48–49 **1** 1 An infection is when bacteria or viruses make an animal sick. 2 Ear infections give you earache. 3 Bacteria get into a body on food, air, or broken skin. 4 Some white blood cells hunt, catch, and eat bacteria. 5 Some white blood cells make bacteria weak and easier to catch. **2** 1 Which microbes does dirt on your fingers have in it? Bacteria 2 How do bacteria get into your mouth? When you touch your mouth. 3 What can some bacteria do if they get inside you? They can make you sick. 4 How can you stop bacteria in dirt getting inside your body? By washing your hands before you eat food. **3** 1 false 2 false 3 true 4 true **4** 1 microbes 2 diseases 3 sneezes 4 breathe 5 Antibiotics 6 chemicals 7 invaders: free answers 8 vaccination: free answers

Page 50–51 **1** 1 Foods that give us useful bacteria: fruit, vegetables, brown bread, brown pasta; Foods that don't give us useful bacteria: ice cream, chocolate, French fries **2** 1 They break down your food into sugar. 2 energy 3 By eating fruit, vegetables, brown bread, and brown pasta. 4 By stopping infections from bad bacteria. **3** 1 bad 2 sugar 3 lactic acid 4 cabbage **4** 1 fuel 2 waste 3 biodigested 4 methane 5 oil 6 nutrients **5** free answers

Subject Area

The World of Science & Technology

Topics & Curriculum Links

types of clothes (Technology)
fabrics and materials (Technology; Science)
the clothing industry (Technology; Civics)
fashion (Technology; Art; Civics)
history of clothes (History)
daily life; local customs; jobs (Geography; Civics)
parts of the body (Science)
countries and weather (Geography)

Vocabulary

clothes; materials; parts of the body; daily activities; weather; seasons; jobs; machines; measurements; dates; numbers; countries; nationalities; continents

Grammar

present simple; present continuous; past simple; present perfect; future simple; question forms; imperative; passive; adjectives; prepositions; adverbs

Teaching Ideas

See also pages 6–7 for general ideas that you can adapt. Or go to **www.oup.com/elt/teacher/readanddiscover**

READ & TALK Clothes and Fabrics

After completing Project 1, students collect the information from the class. They can do this by listening to each student giving their information in turn, or by collecting the information in a big chart on the board. They can talk or write about the results like this: *Most / A lot of / Some / A few of the clothes are made of ... / were made in ...*

READ & TALK Fashion Designs

After completing Project 2, students present their fashion designs to the rest of the class. They can write and talk about their designs like this: *This model is wearing ... The ... is ... and it's made of ...* Then they display all the designs together, and students write comments on each other's designs. Students can then vote for their favorite design.

READ & TALK Who Is It?

Describe someone in a photo from the Reader and ask students to guess who, and to say which page, for example: *The person is wearing ... He / She is ...* Students can then do the same activity in pairs or small groups.

Traditional Costumes Research

Students choose a country, and they do research on traditional costumes in that country, using books or the Internet. Then they write about their findings and display the information. Students can work in groups and posters can then be displayed together, by type of clothing, or by country.

Activities Answers

Pages 36–37 **1** 1 hat 2 tie 3 shirt 4 pants 5 coat 6 dress 7 sweater 8 shoes 9 socks 10 scarf **2** 1 People wear their best clothes at weddings. 2 A hat made of wool helps you to stay warm. 3 White clothes help you to stay cool. 4 Rich people often buy expensive clothes. 5 Clothes in the past were big and heavy. 6 Today, people wear light, comfortable clothes. **3** 1 tight 2 country 3 wedding 4 clothes 5 dress 6 factory **4** 1 People wear hats in cold weather to stay warm. 2 Because a wedding is an important day. 3 Because it helps them to stay cool. 4 Because they are made quickly in big factories. **5** free answers

Pages 38–39 **1** 1 purse 2 jacket 3 T-shirt 4 tunic 5 pocket 6 fabric 7 buttons 8 spinning wheel. Secret word: painting **2** 1 tunics 2 clothes 3 paintings 4 pants 5 pieces **3** 1 About 100,000 years ago. 2 Threads woven together into pieces of fabric. 3 The spinning wheel. 4 Their money **4** 1 Adjectives: long, beautiful, big, expensive. Colors: black, blue, green, white. Clothes: dress, hat, shoes, tunic **5 Example answer** The woman is wearing a long green dress.

Pages 40–41 **1** 1 suit 2 coat 3 usually 4 different 5 wool 6 South Korea **2** 1 We can learn about other people if we look at their clothes. 2 Police officers usually wear a uniform. 3 The special clothes of a country are called the traditional costume. 4 The buba is the traditional costume of Mali. 5 Peruvian traditional clothes are usually made of wool. 6 Men's kimonos have simpler sleeves. **3** 1 Farmers don't wear a uniform. 2 Police officers wear a uniform. 3 Newsreaders don't wear a uniform. 4 Pilots wear a uniform. 5 Teachers don't wear a uniform. 6 Movie stars don't wear a uniform. 7 Nurses wear a uniform. 8 Doctors don't wear a uniform. **4** free answers

Pages 42–43 **1** 1 children 2 poor 3 weren't 4 Rompers 5 are 6 uniform **2** 1 stores 2 synthetic 3 bright 4 shoes 5 serious 6 decoration 7 wash 8 babies **3** 1 clothes 2 uniform 3 colors 4 school 5 rompers **4** 1 In factories 2 Because they are cheaper than in the past. 3 Long, white dresses 4 The king of Spain's daughter 5 School uniform 6 Because they are made of loose, light fabric. **5** free answers

Pages 44–45 **1** 1 silk 2 wool 3 wool 4 cotton 5 silk 6 cotton **2** 1 winter 2 China 3 synthetic 4 silkworm 5 sports **3** 1 cotton 2 fabric 3 thread 4 dress **4** 1 grow 2 pick 3 washed 4 threads 5 underwear 6 dry **5** free answers

Pages 46–47 **1** 1 sewing machine 2 buttons 3 zipper 4 factory 5 truck 6 money **2** 1 First, a designer designs some new coats. 2 The design is sent to the factory. 3 A factory worker makes a sample. 4 A model puts on the sample. The buyer and the designer look at it. 5 The buyer sends an order for lots of coats to the factory. 6 The factory makes lots of coats and sends them to a store. 7 A customer buys a coat. **3** 1 ~~Most~~ Some people in the clothing industry are very rich. 2 The ~~customer~~ designer draws the design on paper or on a computer. 3 The design is sent to the ~~store~~ factory. 4 The factory worker ~~buys~~ makes the samples. 5 Some famous designers make a lot of ~~models~~ money. 6 Fairtrade clothes are not made by children. **4** free answers

Pages 48–49 **1** 1 true 2 true 3 false 4 true 5 false 6 true **2** 1 old-fashioned 2 change 3 everybody 4 T-shirts 5 words 6 pockets **3** 1 Fashions change all the time. 2 T-shirts are comfortable and cheap. 3 T-shirts are usually made of cotton. 4 Some jeans have strong pockets because they have rivets. 5 Jeans became very popular when people saw them in movies. **4** 1 He was a famous American singer. 2 They thought they were a new idea. 3 It became a big business. 4 Cotton 5 A strong cotton fabric called *Genoa fustian*. 6 Because the fabric was strong. **5** free answers

Pages 50–51 **1** 1 Models 2 Designers 3 Fashion victims 4 Young people 5 Goths **2** 1 Clothes made by famous designers are very ~~cheap~~ expensive. 2 Designers show their new ~~photos~~ ideas at fashion shows. 3 Designers like seeing photos of their ~~pets~~ clothes in the newspapers. 4 Fashion victims want all the ~~oldest~~ newest fashions. 5 Harajuku is a ~~school uniform~~ street fashion in Japan. **3** 1 Adjectives: amazing, crazy, funny, nice. Sizes: big, little, long, short. Colors: black, orange, pink, white. Clothes: hat, jacket, shoes, skirt **4** free answers **5** 1 uniform 2 fabric 3 synthetic 4 wool 5 jeans 6 rompers

Subject Area

The World of Science & Technology

Topics & Curriculum Links

types of energy (Science)
how energy is converted (Science)
materials and products (Science; Technology)
conductors and insulators (Science)
tools and machines (Technology)
plants and animals (Science)
natural resources (Science)
sound and light (Science)
types of fuel (Science)
pollution; protecting the environment (Science; Civics)
saving energy (Science; Civics)
places and countries (Geography)
quantities and measurements (Mathematics)

Vocabulary

daily activities; products; machines; weather; parts of the body; forms of water; clothes; buildings; animals; materials; transportation; numbers; measurements; countries

Grammar

present simple; present continuous; past simple; future simple; present perfect; question forms; imperative; passive; adjectives; prepositions; adverbs

Teaching Ideas

See also pages 6–7 for general ideas that you can adapt. Or go to **www.oup.com/elt/teacher/readanddiscover**

READ & TALK An Energy Survey
After completing Project 1, students collect the energy information from the class. They can do this by listening to each student giving their information in turn, or by collecting the information in a big version of the chart on page 52 of the Reader. Then they make a class display to show all the different machines that students use, what they use them for, and for how long.

READ & TALK An Energy Debate
After completing Project 2, students work in small groups. Ask each group to think about what is the best way to save energy. Then in turn, each group presents their arguments. The other groups can ask questions and argue back. Give a prize for the most convincing argument!

Activities Answers

Page 36–37 **1** 1 false 2 true 3 true 4 false **2** 1 energy 2 kinetic 3 Wind 4 sailing boats 5 Potential 6 stored **3** 1 When we stretch a rubber band, we give it energy. 2 When we jump on a trampoline, this stretches its springs. 3 When we stretch a trampoline this gives the springs potential energy. 4 When springs can't be stretched any more, potential energy is converted into kinetic energy.
4 1 potential 2 energy 3 kinetic 4 potential 5 kinetic

Page 38–39 **1** 1 Heat energy from the sun makes Earth warm. 2 Inside our body, heat energy keeps us warm. 3 We can use heat energy to make our homes warm. 4 When heat is added to something its temperature gets higher. 5 When something is cold it has a low temperature. **2** 1 atoms 2 molecules 3 small. 4 more **3** 1 solid molecules 2 gas molecules 3 liquid molecules **4** 1 cooler 2 conduction 3 temperature 4 materials 5 wood **5** 1 We have to stop heat moving from the inside to the outside. 2 They stop heat moving from warm places to cold places. 3 Because heat moves slowly through the air. 4 The jacket holds air next to our body and this stops heat leaving our body.

Page 40–41 **1** Things that are transparent: windows, water, air Things that are opaque: walls, trees, doors **2** 1 Sound and light are types of energy that travel in the air. 2 Sound happens when something vibrates. 3 When a drum vibrates, it makes the air around the drum vibrate, too. 4 The vibrations of sound travel through the air in all directions. 5 The vibrations of sound in the air are called sound waves. **3** 1 Sounds lose energy and get ~~stronger~~ weaker when they move. 2 To send sounds from one place to another, ~~light~~ sound waves are converted into radio waves. 3 Radio waves are ~~visible~~ invisible. We ~~can~~ can't see them. 4 Cell phones convert radio waves back into sound waves so that we can ~~see~~ hear the sounds.
4 1 true 2 false 3 true 4 false 5 false 6 true **5** free answers

Page 42–43 **1** 1 fuels 2 potential 3 energy 4 kinetic 5 powders 6 sound 7 first 8 sparks 9 chemicals The secret word is: fireworks
2 1 We use chemical energy from food to live, to move, and to grow. 2 Plants convert light energy from the sun into chemical energy. 3 Plants store chemical energy. 4 Animals eat plants to use some of the chemical energy from the plant. 5 In food chains, energy from food moves from one living thing to another. **3** 1 sun 2 energy 3 dissolves 4 chemicals

Page 44–45 **1** 1 heat energy 2 light energy 3 sound energy 4 kinetic energy **2** 1 electrons 2 electricity 3 lightning 4 movement **3** 1 true 2 false 3 false 4 true 5 true **4** 1 In a toaster, electricity is used to cook bread. 2 Metal wires in a toaster slow down the electricity so that some of its energy is converted into heat. 3 In a hairdryer, electric wires give us heat. 4 Electricity turns a fan to push heat out of a hairdryer to dry hair. 5 In a lamp, electricity makes a wire so hot that it become white and glows. **5** 1 They use batteries. 2 Because they can store electricity. 3 When we turn on a machine. 4 Because the chemicals inside are dangerous.

Page 46–47 **1** 1 fuels 2 coal 3 oil 4 ancient 5 jungles 6 earth 7 heat 8 mud 9 animals 10 plants **2** 1 gas 2 plants 3 oceans 4 miners 5 ground 6 mostly 7 oil **3** 1 What do large power stations use to make electricity? They use the chemical energy in coal. 2 Why do people burn coal in a coal power station? They use the heat energy to boil water. 3 What type of energy does steam from boiling water have? It has kinetic energy. 4 In a power station, what does steam turn? It turns a turbine. 5 How does a turbine help to make electricity? It turns a generator. **4** 1 false 2 true 3 true 4 true

Page 48–49 **1** 1 Fossil fuels are made from plants and animals that lived millions of years ago. 2 Fossil fuels are non-renewable. 3 Oil will run out in 40 to 70 years. 4 Gas will run out in 50 to 150 years.
2 1 Fossil fuels make different gases that make the air ~~clean~~ dirty. 2 Air pollution is ~~good~~ bad for plants, animals, and people. 3 Power stations and vehicles ~~stop~~ make air pollution. 4 Air pollution is worse in cities where there are ~~few~~ many cars. 5 In some cities, people wear a mask over their ~~bicycle~~ face. **3** 1 Heat from the sun warms Earth. 2 Some heat bounces off Earth and goes back into space. 3 Greenhouse gases stop some heat going back into space. 4 Greenhouse gases store heat and keep earth warm.
4 1 air 2 climate 3 warming 4 fires 5 ice 6 uranium 7 invisible

Page 50–51 **1** 1 We need to use fewer fossil fuels. 2 Renewable energy comes from wind, water, and sunlight. 3 Renewable energy will not run out. 4 People use solar energy heat from the sun to warm water. 5 Solar panels in a roof use heat from the sun to warm water. 6 Photovoltaic cells convert sunlight into electricity. **2** 1 air 2 turbines 3 tall 4 blades 5 propeller 6 generator **3** 1 It has kinetic energy. 2 Water turns turbines that turn generators to make electricity. 3 It holds the water. 4 The potential energy is converted into kinetic energy. 5 It makes electricity for about 1.3 million people.
4 free answers

Subject Area

The World of Science & Technology

Topics & Curriculum Links

parts of the body (Science)
inside the body; cells (Science)
how the body works (Science)
healthy eating (Science; Civics)
caring for your body; illness and medicine (Science; Civics)
sizes and measurements (Mathematics)
sports and other hobbies (Civics)

Vocabulary

parts of the body; shapes; food; daily activities; sports; diseases; measurements; numbers

Grammar

present simple; future simple; question forms; imperative; passive; adjectives; prepositions; adverbs

Teaching Ideas

See also pages 6–7 for general ideas that you can adapt. Or go to **www.oup.com/elt/teacher/readanddiscover**

Caring for Your Body

After reading Chapter 8, students design a poster about how to care for your body. Or students work in small groups, and each group designs a poster about one aspect, for example, eating healthy food, doing exercise, resting, keeping clean, protecting your body. Posters can then be displayed together.

READ & TALK A Body Quiz

After completing Project 1, students write more quiz questions. They can work in small groups. Each group writes questions for a different chapter of the Reader, or they can write one question for each chapter. Collect the questions and do the quiz as a whole class.

READ & TALK A Body Presentation

After completing Project 2, students present their poster to the rest of the class. They can write and talk about the part of the body like this: *It looks like ... It's made of ... It ... to keep you healthy. To care for this part of the body, you should ...* Or other students can ask the questions on page 53 of the Reader. Posters can then be displayed together.

Activities Answers

Pages 36–37 1 1 cells 2 things 3 cytoplasm 4 membrane 5 nucleus **2** 1 A human body has ~~about a billion cells~~ more than ten trillion cells. 2 A cell's nucleus is ~~outside~~ inside the membrane. 3 Water ~~can't~~ can go through the cell membrane. 4 Red blood cells are ~~an irregular~~ a round shape. 5 Your muscle cells are ~~short~~ long and thin. **3** 1 The mother produces an egg cell. 2 The egg cell joins with the father's sperm cell. 3 The new cell divides many times to form an embryo. 4 The embryo gets bigger and it's called a fetus. 5 The baby is finally born after about nine months. **4** 1 They weigh about three times more than when they were born. 2 In their first two years. 3 Between the ages of 11 and 15. 4 When they are about 20 years old. 5 They often get lines and wrinkles on their skin. 6 They stop working.

Pages 38–39 1 1 epidermis 2 dermis 3 hair 4 oil gland 5 pore 6 hair follicle 7 sweat gland 8 fat cells **2** 1 Your hair grows from your skin. True 2 The skin on your body is elastic. True 3 Fingernails are made of keratin. True 4 Human hair is made of living cells. False 5 Your hair and skin contain melanin. True. **3** 1 oil 2 melanin 3 toenails 4 pores 5 root 6 head **4** 1 Because their skin is less elastic. 2 When you feel cold. 3 About 2 or 3 millimeters. 4 About 1 millimeter. 5 It helps to cool your body. 6 About 100.

Pages 40–41 1 1 skull 2 rib 3 arm 4 hand 5 hip 6 femur 7 knee 8 foot **2** 1 feet 2 arms 3 hip 4 bones 5 shorter **3** 1 Your ossicles are the smallest bones in your body. 2 The marrow is where your body grows new red blood cells. 3 You have cartilage between the bones in your joints. 4 Your tendons join your muscles to your bones. 5 Involuntary muscles do their work automatically. **4** 1 To stop the ends of the bones touching. 2 The femur. 3 About 100,000 times. 4 Your brain. 5 Protein.

Pages 42–43 1 1 air 2 trachea 3 lung 4 bronchi 5 alveoli 6 bronchioles **2** 1 oxygen 2 waste gas 3 red blood cells 4 tanks 5 asthma 6 lungs **3** Diver: air tank, mouthpiece, underwater; Mountain Climber: oxygen tank, high altitudes, mask **4** 1 false 2 true 3 false 4 true 5 true **5** 1 About 250 million. 2 By using an inhaler. 3 About five million. 4 For a minute or two.

Pages 44–45 1 1 red 2 smaller 3 kidneys 4 back to 5 water **2** 1 The right atrium gets blood from the whole body. 2 The right atrium sends blood to the right ventricle. 3 The right ventricle pumps blood to the lungs. 4 From the lungs, the blood goes to the left atrium. 5 The left atrium sends blood to the left ventricle. 6 The left ventricle pumps blood to the whole body. **3** 1 (clockwise from top right): carbon dioxide, oxygen, proteins, sugar, fats, white blood cells, red blood cells **4** 1 When it has lots of oxygen. 2 Millions. 3 It cleans people's blood. 4 The left side. 5 To help people who are sick and need operations.

Pages 46–47 1 1 esophagus 2 stomach 3 large intestine 4 small intestine 5 pancreas 6 rectum **2** 1 Your body gets nutrients from your food. 2 You use your teeth to bite and chew your food. 3 Your tongue helps to move food around in your mouth. 4 Saliva makes food easier to chew and swallow. 5 Your stomach mixes the food with gastric juices. **3** 1 Meat and fish give you carbohydrates. False 2 Your body uses vitamins for energy. False 3 Your small intestine is about 2 meters long. False 4 Your body doesn't need any fats to grow. False 5 Your pancreas produces a chemical called insulin. True **4** 1 Because they give you vitamins and minerals that you need to stay healthy. 2 It takes away most of the water. 3 To control the amount of sugar in their blood. 4 Your body breaks down most of your food and takes in nutrients. 5 Your esophagus.

Pages 48–49 1 1 protect 2 controls 3 remember 4 damage 5 sends 6 joins 7 receive 8 contains 9 take 10 keep. Secret word: communicate **2** 1 cerebrum 2 cerebellum 3 brain stem 4 spinal cord 5 vertebrae **3** 1 axon 2 brain stem 3 Because the nerve cells in their brain are damaged. 4 vertebrae 5 A long, irregular shape.

Pages 50–51 1 1 platelets 2 scab 3 white blood cells 4 plaster cast 5 high fever 6 sleep **2** 1 New skin cells grow on top of under a scab. 2 There are no germs in the air that we breathe. 3 A plaster cast keeps broken bones smooth straight. 4 When you sweat you help your body to warm up cool down. 5 Your body can grow new bone clots cells. **3** 1 broken 2 infection 3 equipment 4 accident 5 capillaries 6 temperature 7 dangerous 8 bleeding **4** 1 They close. 2 When the cut is healed. 3 To see where a bone is broken. 4 More than 100 years ago. 5 They kill the germs and keep your body healthy.
5 Example answers You can give your body the nutrients it needs. Do exercise to keep your heart, lungs, muscles, and bones strong. Get enough sleep every night so your body can rest.

Subject Area

The Natural World

Topics & Curriculum Links

galaxies and stars (Science)
solar systems, planets, and moons (Science)
quantities, measurements, sizes, temperatures (Mathematics)
astronomy; space exploration (Science; History)
machines (Technology)
materials (Science)
countries (Geography)
dates and events (History)

Vocabulary

outer space; planets; places; materials; gases; weather; machines; dates; numbers; measurements; countries; nationalities; continents

Grammar

present simple; present continuous; past simple; present perfect; past continuous; future simple; question forms; imperative; passive; adjectives; prepositions; adverbs

Teaching Ideas

See also pages 6–7 for general ideas that you can adapt. Or go to **www.oup.com/elt/teacher/readanddiscover**

READ & TALK A Planet Chart

After completing Project 1, students present their planet to the rest of the class. Posters can be displayed together. Students then complete a big chart for all the planets in the solar system, using headings like these: *Name; Size; Distance from the Sun; Temperature; Made of; Orbit; Moons.* They can refer to the Reader, the posters, and other books or the Internet. You can also do a class quiz with the information collected.

READ & TALK A Space Hotel Advert

After completing Project 2, students present their space hotel to the rest of the class. Other students can ask the questions on page 52 of the Reader. Then they display the posters together, and students write comments about the posters. They can then vote for their favorite space hotel.

READ & TALK A Space Debate

Students work in two groups. Ask one group to think about the arguments for living on the Moon and the other group to think about the arguments for living on Earth. Then in turn each group presents their arguments, like this: *You can ... There is a lot of ... There isn't any ... It's easy to ...* The other group can argue back with arguments against. Give a prize for the most convincing argument.

Activities Answers

Pages 36–37 1 1 galaxy 2 solar 3 orbit 4 axis **2** 1 giants 2 stars 3 helium 4 dwarf 5 axis 6 energy. Secret word: galaxy **3** 1 dwarf planet 2 planet 3 star 4 solar system 5 galaxy 6 universe **4** 1 billion 2 the Sun 3 rocks 4 billion 5 heat **5** 1 When a place on Earth is opposite the Sun. 2 Nuclear fusion. 3 It gives them energy to grow. 4 Because they travel a shorter distance. 5 Eris, and it's 2,500 kilometers across.

Pages 38–39 1 1 Mercury 2 Venus 3 Earth 4 Mars; 1 Mars 2 Venus 3 Mercury 4 Earth 5 Venus 6 Mars **2** 1 true 2 false 3 true 4 false 5 true 6 false **3** 1 temperature 2 atmosphere 3 canyon 4 carbon dioxide 5 pressure 6 sulphuric acid **4** 1 rocks and soil 2 sulphuric acid 3 Because it has liquid water. 4 27 days 5 Because of chemicals 6 rivers

Pages 40–41 1 1 Mercury 2 Venus 3 Earth 4 Mars 5 Jupiter 6 Saturn 7 Uranus 8 Neptune **2** 1 ring 2 cloud 3 lake 4 storm 5 ice 6 rock **3** 1 liquid 2 storm 3 chemicals 4 rings 5 second **4** 1 The outer planets are called the gas giants. 2 Titan is one of Saturn's moons. 3 Jupiter is the biggest planet in the solar system. 4 Saturn's rings are made of ice. 5 Neptune is the farthest planet from the Sun. 6 Uranus has 27 moons. **5** 1 Gas giants are bigger and they're made of gases, not rocks. 2 Because of chemicals in the ice. 3 Because it's far from the Sun.

Pages 42–43 1 1 comet 2 asteroid 3 meteor 4 meteorite **2** 1 rings 2 rocks 3 ice 4 tail 5 burn 6 crater 7 dinosaurs **3** 1 C 2 T 3 C 4 C 5 T 6 C 7 T **4** 1 The asteroid belt is between ~~Earth~~ Mars and the ~~Sun~~ Jupiter. 2 A lot of comets come from the ~~asteroid~~ Kuiper belt. 3 Comets become ~~colder~~ hotter when they are near the Sun. 4 We can see Halley's Comet in the sky ~~all the time~~ every 75 or 76 years. 5 Some meteorites hit the ~~Moon~~ Jupiter in 1994. 6 About 65 million years ago, there were no ~~animals~~ people on Earth.

Pages 44–45 1 1 temple 2 calendar 3 seeds 4 telescope 5 spacecraft 6 astronomer **2** 1 prove 2 festival 3 believe 4 temple 5 explore 6 calculate 7 force **3** 1 sun, believed 2 believed, important 3 gravity, proved 4 discovered, universe **4** 1 true 2 true 3 true 4 false 5 false **5** 1 free answers

Pages 46–47 1 1 canal 2 alien 3 bacteria 4 UFO **2** 1 Earth, Mars, Titan 2 Mars, Europa 3 Mars 4 Earth, Titan 5 Earth **3** 1 simple 2 imagine 3 underground 4 covers **4** 1 liquid 2 Mars 3 warmer 4 hydrocarbons **5** 1 Because astronomers thought that they saw lines on the surface. 2 Because it's so cold that all the water is ice. 3 Hydrocarbons and water 4 free answers

Pages 48–49 1 1957 rocket, 1961 person, 1968 orbited, 1969 Moon, 1981 space shuttle, 1998 Space Station **2** 1 false 2 true 3 false 4 true 5 true 6 false **3** 1 float 2 sleeping bag 3 gravity 4 exercise 5 mask 6 shower 7 containers 8 weak **4** free answers

Pages 50–51 1 1 space suit 2 Radiation 3 experiments 4 Engineers **2** 1 Space planes are cheaper than rockets. 2 Robonauts go to dangerous places. 3 Earth's atmosphere protects us from radiation. 4 Maybe tourists will stay in space hotels. 5 Scientists will probably invent faster spacecraft. **3** 1 This has happened: robots on Mars, space planes, space tourism; This will happen: a Moon base, very fast new spacecraft, astronauts on Mars; Maybe this will happen one day: space hotels, finding aliens, exploring other solar systems **4** 1 Special space planes. 2 In about 2020. 3 Because radiation isn't a problem for them. 4 free answers

Caring for Our Planet

Subject Area

The Natural World

Topics & Curriculum Links

the importance of water (Science; Civics)
conserving energy and natural resources (Science; Civics)
reducing waste and pollution (Science; Civics)
dangers in the environment (Geography; Civics)
weather and changing climates (Geography)
plants and animals (Science)
machines, energy, and fuels (Technology)
transportation (Technology)
food chains (Science)
protecting plants and animals (Science; Civics)
places and countries (Geography)
dates and events (History)

Vocabulary

natural resources; places; animals; plants; daily routines; food; weather; climate; fuels; energy; transportation; machines; materials; dates; numbers; measurements; countries; continents

Grammar

present simple; present continuous; past simple; present perfect; future simple; question forms; imperative; passive; adjectives; prepositions; adverbs

Teaching Ideas

See also pages 6–7 for general ideas that you can adapt. Or go to **www.oup.com/elt/teacher/readanddiscover**

Electricity Research

After reading Chapter 3, students do research about how electricity is made in their country, using books or the Internet. They can also do research about how much electricity comes from different sources, for example, coal, gas, nuclear. They can also do this for other countries as a comparison. Then they present their findings on a poster, using charts and diagrams.

READ & TALK City or Village Life?

After reading Chapter 8, students work in two groups. Ask one group to think about the arguments for living in a city and the other group to think about the arguments for living in a village. Then in turn each group presents their arguments, like this: *You can ... There is a lot of ... There isn't any ... It's easy to ...* The other group can argue back with arguments against. Give a prize for the most convincing arguments!

Caring for Our Planet Poster

Students design a poster about how to care for our planet. Or students work in small groups, and each group designs a poster about one topic, for example, energy, pollution, plants, animals. Posters can then be displayed together. Students can vote for their favorite design.

Activities Answers

Pages 36–37 **1** 1 sun ✓ 2 water ✓ 3 oil 4 plants ✓ 5 coal 6 animals ✓ **2** 1 renewable 2 water 3 fresh 4 fossil fuels 5 electricity 6 pollution **3 Example answers** Things that use electricity: computers. Things that don't use electricity: bicycles **4** 1 Renewable resources can replace themselves naturally. 2 Plants, animals, and people all need water to live. 3 They have to travel a long way to collect water, or move to a new place. 4 We can keep it clean and not waste it. 5 They cannot be replaced so one day they will run out. 6 free answers

Pages 38–39 **1** 1 USA 2 Sahara Desert 3 Bangladesh 4 Gobi Desert 5 South Korea 6 China 7 Australia 8 Tuvalu 9 New Zealand **2** 1 sun 2 gases 3 warm 4 fossil fuels 5 greenhouse effect 6 carbon dioxide **3** 1 true 2 false 3 true 4 false 5 true 6 true **4** 1 Carbon dioxide increases the greenhouse effect. 2 Scientists think that global warming is changing our climate. 3 Parts of Funafati are only 10 centimeters above sea level. 4 Our planet has natural ways to reduce carbon dioxide. 5 By using fewer fossil fuels and producing less carbon dioxide.

Pages 40–41 **1** Geothermal energy: underground heat, hot water, steam; Wind energy: wind farms, wind turbines, colder countries; Energy from Water: rivers, lakes, ocean waves, ocean tides; Solar Energy: sunshine, solar panels, sunny countries **2** 1 sun 2 radioactive waste 3 water 4 water 5 China **3** 1 Nuclear waste is not safe for thousands of years. 2 In Ukraine, 336,000 people had to move to new homes. 3 We can use solar panels to power watches and calculators. 4 Wind energy is very useful in colder countries. 5 Hot water and steam from underground can heat buildings. 6 We can make electricity from ocean waves and tides. **4** 1 In places where it's very sunny all year long. 2 We can use water from rivers, lakes or oceans. 3 free answers

Pages 42–43 **1** 1 short 2 less 3 solar energy 4 cleaner 5 plants 6 bigger **2** Good for Earth: catalytic converters, cycling, walking, carbon offsetting, biofuels; Bad for Earth: big cars, planes, pollution, exhaust gases **3** 1 power 2 clean 3 solar 4 cars 5 biofuels 6 planes 7 big 8 cycle 9 dirty 10 trees. Secret word: passengers **4** free answers

Pages 44–45 **1** Recycle: newspapers, parts of cars, glass containers, empty cans, plastic containers, clothes; Make into compost: garden waste, food waste **2** 1 true 2 true 3 false 4 false 5 false 6 true **3** 1 Pollution is dangerous for animals. 2 About a billion people do not have clean water. 3 Many people now recycle a lot of waste. 4 Waste from factories can pollute water. 5 We can try to reuse more things. **4** 1 By waste from factories and human waste. 2 By using a compost bin. 3 Because there are too many, and it's difficult to recycle them. 4 free answers 5 free answers

Pages 46–47 **1** grass, cow, person; corn, mouse, owl; lettuce, rabbit, fox; plant plankton, fish, sea lion, killer whale **2** 1 false 2 true 3 false 4 true 5 true 6 false **3** 1 Many useful plants grow in rainforests. 2 We are using too many trees. 3 Fish eat plant plankton. 4 We make flour from wheat and corn. 5 We all need plants. **4** 1 They need sunlight, water, and carbon dioxide. 2 Olive oil. 3 For wood to make furniture or paper, or to make space to grow crops, or to raise cattle. 4 By keeping our planet clean, by using fewer fossil fuels to reduce global warming, by using fewer trees, by planting new trees.

Pages 48–49 **1** 1 chicken 2 flies 3 ant 4 elephant 5 panda 6 cow 7 bee 8 gorilla 9 polar bear 10 beetle 11 sheep 12 whale **2** 1 animals 2 fish farms 3 eggs 4 nectar, honey 5 work 6 compost **3** 1 hunters 2 habitat 3 rare 4 pollution 5 feathers 6 rainforest 7 whale 8 cows **4** 1 When we cut down rainforest tree we destroy habitats. 2 If the ice at the North Pole melts, polar bears will be in danger. 3 Elephants were hunted because people could sell their tusks. 4 Rainforests are the natural habitat of gorillas and tigers. 5 Animals are safe in safari parks.

Pages 50–51 **1** Problems for our planet: 1 energy 2 waste 3 transport; How we can care for our planet: 4 greedy 5 less 6 food 7 reuse 8 electricity **2** 1 protect: damage, 32 2 increase: reduce, 35 3 old: new, 33 4 near: far, 32, 34 5 cold: hot, 33 6 summer: winter, 34 **3** 1 It's important to remember to turn off lights. 2 It's good to eat fruit from your own country. 3 It's good to reuse and recycle things as much as possible. 4 We can help the planet in small ways. **4** 1, 2 & 3 free answers

Subject Area

The Natural World

Topics & Curriculum Links

history of Earth (Science, History)
materials and natural resources (Science; Civics)
types of rock; the rock cycle (Geography)
how Earth moves (Geography)
plants and animals; classification (Science)
parts of the body (Science)
natural processes (Science)
weather and changing climates (Geography)
protecting the environment (Science; Civics)
places and countries (Geography)
dates and events (History)
quantities and measurements (Mathematics)

Vocabulary

numbers; materials; forms of water; weather; plants; parts of plants: food; seasons; animals; parts of the body, places; buildings; measurements; countries; continents

Grammar

present simple; present continuous; past simple; present perfect; question forms; imperative; passive; adjectives; prepositions; adverbs

Teaching Ideas

See also pages 6–7 for general ideas that you can adapt. Or go to **www.oup.com/elt/teacher/readanddiscover**

READ & TALK A National Park Presentation

After completing Project 1, students present their national park to the rest of the class. Posters can then be displayed together, organizing them by type of national park, or by continent.

READ & TALK An Earth Quiz

After completing Project 2, students write more quiz questions. They can work in small groups. Each group writes questions for a different chapter of the Reader, or they can write one question for each chapter. Collect the questions and do the quiz as a whole class.

READ & TALK An Earth Time Line

Students create a time line to show the history of Earth. They can divide the time line into units of 100 million years, from 0 years ago (today) to 600 million years ago. Then students re-read the Reader and write important events on the time line. A large version can be displayed in class.

Activities Answers

Page 36–37 **1** 1 false 2 true 3 true 4 false **2** 1 energy 2 kinetic 3 Wind 4 sailing boats 5 Potential 6 stored **3** 1 When we stretch a rubber band, we give it energy. 2 When we jump on a trampoline, this stretches its springs. 3 When we stretch a trampoline this gives the springs potential energy. 4 When springs can't be stretched any more, potential energy is converted into kinetic energy. **4** 1 potential 2 energy 3 kinetic 4 potential 5 kinetic

Page 38–39 **1** 1 Heat energy from the sun makes Earth warm. 2 Inside our body, heat energy keeps us warm. 3 We can use heat energy to make our homes warm. 4 When heat is added to something its temperature gets higher. 5 When something is cold it has a low temperature. **2** 1 atoms 2 molecules 3 small. 4 more **3** 1 solid molecules 2 gas molecules 3 liquid molecules **4** 1 cooler 2 conduction 3 temperature 4 materials 5 wood **5** 1 We have to stop heat moving from the inside to the outside. 2 They stop heat moving from warm places to cold places. 3 Because heat moves slowly through the air. 4 The jacket holds air next to our body and this stops heat leaving our body.

Page 40–41 **1** Things that are transparent: windows, water, air Things that are opaque: walls, trees, doors **2** 1 Sound and light are types of energy that travel in the air. 2 Sound happens when something vibrates. 3 When a drum vibrates, it makes the air around the drum vibrate, too. 4 The vibrations of sound travel through the air in all directions. 5 The vibrations of sound in the air are called sound waves. **3** 1 Sounds lose energy and get ~~stronger~~ weaker when they move. 2 To send sounds from one place to another, ~~light~~ sound waves are converted into radio waves. 3 Radio waves are ~~visible~~ invisible. We ~~can~~ can't see them 4 Cell phones convert radio waves back into sound waves so that we can ~~see~~ hear the sounds. **4** 1 true 2 false 3 true 4 false 5 false 6 true **5** free answers

Page 42–43 **1** 1 fuels 2 potential 3 energy 4 kinetic 5 powders 6 sound 7 first 8 sparks 9 chemicals The secret word is: fireworks **2** 1 We use chemical energy from food to live, to move, and to grow. 2 Plants convert light energy from the sun into chemical energy. 3 Plants store chemical energy. 4 Animals eat plants to use some of the chemical energy from the plant. 5 In food chains, energy from food moves from one living thing to another. **3** 1 sun 2 energy 3 dissolves 4 chemicals

Page 44–45 **1** 1 heat energy 2 light energy 3 sound energy 4 kinetic energy **2** 1 electrons 2 electricity 3 lightning 4 movement **3** 1 true 2 false 3 false 4 true 5 true **4** 1 In a toaster, electricity is used to cook bread. 2 Metal wires in a toaster slow down the electricity so that some of its energy is converted into heat. 3 In a hairdryer, electric wires give us heat. 4 Electricity turns a fan to push heat out of a hairdryer to dry hair. 5 In a lamp, electricity makes a wire so hot that it become white and glows **5** 1 They use batteries. 2 Because they can store electricity. 3 When we turn on a machine. 4 Because the chemicals inside are dangerous.

Page 46–47 **1** 1 fuels 2 coal 3 oil 4 ancient 5 jungles 6 earth 7 heat 8 mud 9 animals 10 plants **2** 1 gas 2 plants 3 oceans 4 miners 5 ground 6 mostly 7 oil **3** 1 What do large power stations use to make electricity? They use the chemical energy in coal. 2 Why do people burn coal in a coal power station? They use the heat energy to boil water. 3 What type of energy does steam from boiling water have? It has kinetic energy. 4 In a power station, what does steam turn? It turns a turbine. 5 How does a turbine help to make electricity? It turns a generator. **4** 1 false 2 true 3 true 4 true

Page 48–49 **1** 1 Fossil fuels are made from plants and animals that lived millions of years ago. 2 Fossil fuels are non-renewable. 3 Oil will run out in 40 to 70 years. 4 Gas will run out in 50 to 150 years. **2** 1 Fossil fuels make different gases that make the air clean dirty. 2 Air pollution is good bad for plants, animals, and people. 3 Power stations and vehicles stop make air pollution. 4 Air pollution is worse in cities where there are few many cars. 5 In some cities, people wear a mask over their bicycle face. **3** 1 Heat from the sun warms Earth. 2 Some heat bounces off Earth and goes back into space. 3 Greenhouse gases stop some heat going back into space. 4 Greenhouse gases store heat and keep earth warm. **4** 1 air 2 climate 3 warming 4 fires 5 ice 6 uranium 7 invisible

Page 50–51 **1** 1 We need to use fewer fossil fuels. 2 Renewable energy comes from wind, water, and sunlight. 3 Renewable energy will not run out. 4 People use solar energy heat from the sun to warm water. 5 Solar panels in a roof use heat from the sun to warm water. 6 Photovoltaic cells convert sunlight into electricity. **2** 1 air 2 turbines 3 tall 4 blades 5 propeller 6 generator **3** 1 It has kinetic energy. 2 Water turns turbines that turn generators to make electricity. 3 It holds the water. 4 The potential energy is converted into kinetic energy. 5 It makes electricity for about 1.3 million people. **4** free answers

Subject Area

The Natural World

Topics & Curriculum Links

types of ecosystem (Science)
plants and animals; classification (Science)
food chains (Science)
parts of the body (Science)
weather and changing climates (Science; Geography)
protecting the environment (Science; Civics)
places and countries (Geography)
dates and events (History)

Vocabulary

plants; animals; parts of the body; places; weather; food; seasons; numbers; measurements; continents

Grammar

present simple; present continuous; past simple; future simple; question forms; imperative; passive; adjectives; prepositions; adverbs

Teaching Ideas

See also pages 6–7 for general ideas that you can adapt. Or go to **www.oup.com/elt/teacher/readanddiscover**

READ & TALK Guess the Ecosystem

Choose one of the ecosystems from the Reader, and without saying its name, read out one sentence about it and ask students to guess which ecosystem it is. Read out more sentences, one at a time, until students guess the correct ecosystem. You can use a point scoring system, for example, five points after one fact, three points after two facts, etc. Students can then do this in small groups.

READ & TALK A New Ecosystem Presentation

After completing Project 2, students present their new ecosystem to the rest of the class. They can describe the ecosystem, or other students can ask the questions on page 53 of the Reader.

Ecosystems in My Country

Using books or the Internet, students do research about different ecosystems in their country. They can write about the climate and geographical features, and about what plants and animals live in the ecosystems, and how they adapt to living there. They can also draw food chains.

Activities Answers

Page 36–37 **1** **1** living **2** animals **3** air **4** ecosystem **5** sunlight **6** decomposers **2** **1**1 grass **2** grasshopper **3** snake **4** buzzard **3** **1** different sizes **2** an ocean **3** a pond **4** different **4** **1** Because bamboo is the only food that they eat. **2** Yes, they can. **3** They have long arms and legs for climbing trees in a forest. **4** They have thick fur to keep them warm. **5** free answers

Page 38–39 **1** **1** A desert is a place that's very ~~wet~~ dry. **2** A hot desert is ~~an easy~~ a difficult place to live in. **3** ~~No~~ Some plants or and animals are adapted to desert ecosystems. **4** Cactus plant stems become ~~thin~~ fat when they are full of water. **5** Desert food chains start with ~~animals~~ plants. **6** Animals that hunt and eat ~~plants~~ other animals are called predators. **2** **1** crickets, desert bats, meerkats **2** scorpions, lizards, hawks, snakes, foxes, meerkats **3** **1** true **2** false **3** true **4** false **5** true **6** true **4** **1** It's an animal that's busy at night and sleeps in the day. **2** Because it's cooler then. **3** They break off the tail first. **4** They hide in burrows. **5** To help them to see at night. **6** So they can hear small animals that they hunt in the dark.

Page 40–41 **1** **1** Grasslands are places with many types of grass and few trees. **2** Grasslands are often found between deserts and forests. **3** Grasses have long roots that go down into the soil and collect water. **4** The leaves of grasses grow from the bottom of the plant, not the top. **2** **1** grasshopper **2** zebra **3** cheetah **4** snake **5** butterfly **6** gazelle **7** rabbit **8** termites **9** kangaroo **10** lion **3** **1** The soil, plants, and animals in grasslands live and work together. **2** When prairie dogs eat tall plants, sunlight can help small plants to grow. **3** Prairie dog droppings add nutrients to the soil. **4** Prairie dog tunnels let air and water into the soil. **4** **1** decomposers **2** nests **3** nutrients **4** plants **5** grassland

Page 42–43 **1** **1** Conifer trees have ~~blue~~ green leaves that look like thin, soft hard spikes. **2** Conifer leaves don't lose as much heat water as flat leaves do. **3** Most conifer trees ~~only have leaves for part of the year.~~ have leaves all year long. **4** It's usually light dark on the forest floor and ~~many~~ few plants grow there. **5** ~~Wolves~~ Birds and squirrels eat seeds from cones that fall from conifer trees. **2** free answers **3** **1** They grow in hot, rainy places. **2** Because they get lots of water, sunlight, and warm air. **3** To help the trees to stand up. **4** They live in the trees. **5** They eat fruit, nuts, and leaves. **4** **1** leaves **2** vole **3** raccoon **4** cougar

Page 44–45 **1** **1** freshwater **2** light **3** roots **4** long **2** **1** Fish are perfectly adapted to living underwater. **2** Fish have gills that get oxygen from the water. **3** Fish have tail fins to help them to swim. **4** Many fish feed on insects and other minibeasts. **5** Some large fish catch and eat other fish. **6** Nutrients from dead animals go back into the freshwater ecosystem. **3** **1** freshwater **2** hatch **3** become **4** insects **5** young **6** adults **7** water **8** beetle **9** swims The secret word is ecosystem. **4** free answers

Page 46–47 **1** **1** Ocean ecosystems are ~~not~~ very important. **2** The coast is the area of ~~water~~ land next to an ocean. **3** Water moves onto a beach and goes out again because of the ~~seaweed~~ tides. **4** Some animals have ~~hats~~ shells that protect them from predators. **2** **1** Coral reefs grow near coasts in cold places. False Corals are soft plants that have a hard skeleton. False After they die, coral skeletons become a coral reef. True **4** Some coral reefs are more than 50 million years old! True **3** **1** At the Top of the Ocean – plankton, shrimps In Deep Water firefly squid, blue whale, anglerfish **4** **1** Tiny plants called plant plankton. **2** Tiny animals, like shrimps. **3** Larger fish, like mackerel. **4** Even larger fish like tuna, or dolphins. **5** The great white shark. **6** Because there's no light there.

Page 48–49 **1** **1** Frozen ecosystems in polar areas are cold and ~~wet~~ dry. **2** Tundra ecosystems near the ~~South~~ North Pole are places that have long, cold winters. **3** Polar bears grow very ~~thin~~ fat in fall and then they hibernate. **4** Seals have ~~arms~~ flippers to help them to swim under the ice. **2** **1** plant plankton **2** shrimp **3** seal **4** polar bear **3** **1** never **2** summer **3** small **4** start **4** **1** true **2** false **3** false **4** true **5** true **5** free answers

Page 50–51 **1** **1** When people change one part of an ecosystem, they can damage other parts of it. **2** People cut down trees for wood, and they clear grassland to build homes. **3** Without plants to use for homes and food, animals in an ecosystem move away or die. **4** Oil pollution is dangerous for ocean ecosystems. **2** **1** They damage ocean food chains. **2** They can kill animals that already live there. **3** It's the way temperatures on Earth are slowly becoming warmer. **4** Because gases from factories, cars, and machines are changing Earth's atmosphere. **5** When oceans get too warm, corals slowly die. **3** **1** Many species of animal will die if we destroy coral reefs. **2** Rainforest plants give people food, medicines, and oxygen. **3** Conservation groups help ecosystems around the world. **4** Some rainforests have guards to stop people cutting down trees. **5** There are areas of water where fisherman can't go fishing. **4** free answers

6 Food Around the World

Subject Area

The World of Arts & Social Studies

Topics & Curriculum Links

food (Science)
healthy eating (Science; Civics)
history of some foods (Geography; History)
typical dishes (Geography; Civics)
food festivals (Geography; Civics)
hunger and lack of food (Civics)
plants and animals (Science)
countries (Geography)

Vocabulary

fruits and vegetables; dairy products; meat and fish; pulses; nutrients; food production; drinks; typical dishes; desserts; street food; measurements; dates; numbers; countries; nationalities continents

Grammar

present simple; past simple; question forms; passive; imperative; adjectives; prepositions; adverbs

Teaching Ideas

See also pages 6–7 for general ideas that you can adapt. Or go to **www.oup.com/elt/teacher/readanddiscover**

READ & TALK A Balanced Diet

After reading Chapter 1, students plan a balanced diet for a week, and write or talk about what they will eat and why. like this: *On Monday, I'm going to eat ... because ... [Foods] are good sources of / have lots of proteins / carbohydrates / fats / minerals / vitamins. You need ... for / to ...*

READ & TALK A Food Festival Presentation

After completing Project 2, students present their festival to the rest of the class. They can write and talk about it like this: *[Festival] is in [places / month] ... We / People celebrate this festival because ... We / They eat ... We / They also ...*

Food Research

Students choose a country and do research, using books or the Internet, to find out about traditional dishes, food festivals, or what food is produced there or imported. Or they can do research on a particular food, for example, rice or sugar, and find out where it is produced, what it is used for, etc. Students then write about their findings and display the information. They can work in groups, and posters can then be displayed together.

Activities Answers

Pages 36–37 **1** 1 energy 2 muscles 3 oils 4 diseases 5 calcium **2** 1 Rice gives us carbohydrates. 2 Eggs give us protein and vitamins. 3 Oranges give us vitamins. 4 Broccoli give us vitamins. Carrots give us vitamins. Honey gives us sugar. **3** 1 from naturally sweet foods. 2 fats for extra energy. 3 to grow healthy hair. 4 our skin healthy. 5 for healthy food. 6 can be bad for our health. **4** 1 Because our bodies digest sugar quickly. 2 Pulses, grains, nuts, and seeds give us proteins. 3 We get proteins and fats from nuts and seeds. 4 Because vitamin C helps to fight diseases. 5 We can get vitamin B from meat and fish. 6 Dairy products are good sources of calcium. **5** free answer

Pages 38–39 **1** Arable Farmers: wheat, cherries, vegetables; Livestock Farmers: dairy products, eggs, meat; Fishermen: tuna, trout, prawns **2** (any order) Arable farmers grow crops. Fruit is grown in fields and orchards. Livestock farmers raise animals. Some fishermen catch seafood. Some plants need lots of water. **3** 1 plow 2 hand 3 pastures 4 paddy fields 5 rivers 6 fish farms **4** 1 They are grown in fields. 2 Fruits are grown on trees in orchards. 3 Cows and sheep produce dairy products. 4 Because this keeps them together and protects them. 5 They have freezers to keep the fish cold. **5** 1 wet fields p9; 2 artificial ponds p11; 3 modern machines p8; 4 saltwater fish p11; 5 flat areas p9

Pages 40–41 **1** 1 iced desserts 2 America 3 1850 4 bitter 5 thinner **2** 1 1843 ice cream 2 1948 popcorn 3 1867 milk chocolate 4 1853 potato chips **3** 1 Chocolate was invented in China. False 2 The world's first popcorn was made in America. True 3 Modern ice cream was invented in Central America. False 4 Hot chocolate became very popular in Spain. True 5 Thin potato chips were invented in Baltimore. False **4** 1 They brought ice and snow from the mountains. 2 Because they were too thick. 3 They cooked popcorn over the fire. 4 Because they had to keep mixing the cream by hand. 5 They added chilli peppers and water.

Pages 42–43 **1** 1 Couscous and tajine are typical foods in Morocco. 2 Pasta and pizza are typical foods in Italy. 3 Kimchi and rice are typical foods in Korea. 4 Tortilla and mole poblano are typical foods in Mexico. **2** 1 false 2 true 3 false 4 true 5 true 6 false **3** 1 They are cooked in a hot pan. 2 They are a star shape. 3 They eat kimchi everyday. 4 They eat tajine with couscous or bread. 5 You can fold them to keep food inside. **4** 1 thick 2 spicy 3 spiral 4 flat 5 hot 6 sweet **5** free answer

Pages 44–45 **1** 1 seed pods 2 sugar 3 yogurt 4 ice 5 baobab fruit 6 tiger nuts **2** 1 horchata, nuts 2 juice, seed pods 3 drink, fruit 4 Indian, yogurt **3** 1 Sweet lassi has sugar in it. 2 Mexican horchata is made with rice. 3 Baobab fruit is also called monkey's bread. 4 Tamarind seed pods are large and brown. 5 Some people add cinnamon to horchata. 6 Tamarind juice can be quite sour. **4** 1 It's most popular in summer. 2 It comes from the bark of cinnamon trees. 3 Because it's very refreshing. 4 People drink tamarind juice in Egypt. 5 They grow underground.

Pages 46–47 **1** 1 Brazilian, cheese bread 2 Turkish, a cherry drink 3 Belgian, French fries 4 Brazilian, palm berry juice 5 Thai, barbecued meat **2** 1 It's Brazilian cheese bread. 2 It's a Turkish cherry drink 3 They are Belgian French fires. 4 It's Brazilian palm berry juice. 5 They are Thai barbecued meats. **3** 1 sugar 2 boats 3 sauces 4 bread 5 dessert **4** 1 What can you have for dessert in Brazil? You can have fresh fruit or sweet coconut pastries. 2 Where do Thai vendors sell fried fishcakes? They sell them on the street. 3 What do Belgian people put on their waffles? They put ice cream, chocolate, fruit, or cream on top. 4 Where can you buy *simit* rings? You can buy them from street carts. 5 What do Thai people put on sticky rice? They put peanuts on it. **5** free answer

Pages 48–49 **1** 1 avocado milkshake, durian fruit 2 maple syrup 3 custard, trifle 4 lucuma fruit **2** 1 sap 2 avocados 3 orange 4 pudding 5 purple 6 strong **3** 1 buckets 2 cake 3 chocolate 4 corn 5 cream 6 ice cream **4** 1 They collect it in early spring. 2 Because durians have a very strong smell. 3 Cake, custard, fruit, and jelly. 4 It has a sweet, nutty flavour. 5 You can see a red maple leaf. 6 free answer

Pages 50–51 **1** 1 India 2 Korea 3 USA 4 Ghana **2** 1 yams 2 rice cakes 3 curry 4 pumpkin pie 5 turkey 6 lentils **3** 1 yams 2 Korea 3 turkey 4 women 5 pumpkin 6 April **4** 1 ancestors 2 parades 3 games 4 pie 5 temples 6 crop **5** 1 They are filled with beans or sesame seeds. 2 It's on the fourth day of November. 3 They go to the cemetery. 4 They wear bright clothes. 5 They watch American football on television. 6 free answer

Subject Area

The World of Arts & Social Studies

Topics & Curriculum Links

jobs and professions (Civics)
charities; voluntary work (Civics)
emergencies (Geography; Civics)
weather and changing climates (Geography)
caring for plants and animals; protecting the environment (Science; Civics)
natural resources; the importance of water (Science; Civics)
health and medicine (Science; Civics)
education (Civics)
daily life (Civics)
where food comes from; food shortages (Geography; Civics)
places and countries (Geography)
dates and events (History)
quantities and measurements (Mathematics)

Vocabulary

jobs; school subjects; languages; food; materials; animals; plants; places; dates; numbers; measurements; countries

Grammar

present simple; present continuous; past simple; future simple; present perfect; past perfect; question forms; imperative; passive; adjectives; prepositions; adverbs

Teaching Ideas

See also pages 6–7 for general ideas that you can adapt. Or go to **www.oup.com/elt/teacher/readanddiscover**

READ & TALK The Most Important Job

After completing Project 1, students present their job that helps others to the rest of the class. Posters can then be displayed together, and students vote for the most important job.

READ & TALK Helping Our Planet Debate

After completing Project 2, students work in small groups. Ask each group to think about what is the most important thing that we can do to help our planet. Then in turn, each group presents their arguments. The other groups can ask questions and argue back. Give a prize for the most convincing argument!

READ & TALK A Helping Interview

Students interview someone about people who help others. They can ask questions like this: *Tell me about someone who helped you (at an important time in your life). What was your problem? How did the person help you?* Alternatively, students can do the interview in their own language, but they write or talk about their interview in English, like this: *... was very sick in hospital. ... helped her to get better.*

Activities Answers

Page 36–37 **1** 1 government 2 Midwives 3 Surgeons 4 dentist 5 volunteer **2** 1 doctor 2 care worker 3 midwife 4 dentist 5-8 free answers **3** 1 A doctor helps someone who is sick. 2 A hospice worker helps people at the end of their life. 3 A dentist cares for someone's teeth. 4 A midwife helps a baby to be born. 5 A care worker cares for someone at home or at a care home. **4 Example answers** 1 People get help from doctors when they are sick. 2 in clinics or hospitals 3 They work with doctors, give medication, and care for sick people. 4 To care for their teeth and mouth. 5 Anyone can do voluntary work.

Page 38–39 **1** 1 mathematics 2 science 3 art 4 languages 5 Information Technology 6 history 7 geography **2** free answers **3** 1 Education 2 teachers 3 assistants 4 university 5 information 6 volunteer **4 Example answers** 1 parents and other people in their family 2 To read and write, and to do art and simple mathematics. 3 They help children to stay safe in the playground. 4 professors 5 free answers

Page 40–41 **1** 1 food 2 garden 3 Farmers 4 rice 5 fruits 6 charities **2** 1 Crops: rice, sugar cane, wheat, corn; Fruits: apples, oranges, bananas; Vegetables: potatoes, onions, carrots **3** 1 food 2 Europe 3 Brazil 4 oranges 5 animals 6 supermarkets 7 seeds **4 Example answers** 1 Because it has lots of important nutrients. 2 in a garden or on other land 3 sugar cane, corn, rice, and wheat 4 chicken and beef 5 more than one billion people

Page 42–43 **1** 1 water 2 clothes 3 home 4 water 5 wells 6 shower **2** 1 water 2 industry 3 wash 4 reservoirs 5 pipes 6 industry 7 safe 8 shower **3 Example answers** 1 To make things and to help machines to work. 2 from rivers, lakes, or under the ground 3 To provide water in places where there isn't enough. 4 People need clean water to stay healthy. 5 about six billion 6 more than one billion **4** free answers **5** free answers

Page 44–45 **1** 1 emergency 2 earthquake 3 refugee camp 4 government 5 international 6 tsunami **2** 1 emergency 2 help 3 refugees 4 camps 5 hurt 6 clothes 7 earthquake, tsunami 8 disaster **3** 1 Some emergencies are because of war. True 2 There aren't many refugees in the world. False 3 A refugee's life is very easy. False 4 About 250,000 homes were destroyed in Haiti. True 5 Dogs helped to rescue people. True **4 Example answers** 1 charities 2 wood and stones 3 January 12th 2010 4 more than a million 5 They helped get food and clean water to everyone, and medicines to people who were sick, and made refugee camps for people who had lost their homes.

Page 46–47 **1** 1 toad 2 fish 3 hamster 4 whale 5 cat 6 bird 7 snow leopard 8 orang-utan **2** free answers **3** 1 There are many more animals than people. 2 Some people give money to adopt an animal. 3 Vets care for animals. 4 Some vets work in veterinary centers. 5 Snow leopards are very rare. 6 There are lots of animal charities. **4 Example answers** 1 To take them away from dangerous roads to a safer place. 2 They care for them, build homes for them, and feed them. 3 To clean them and care for them. 4 They try to move them into deeper water.

Page 48–49 **1** 1 species 2 extinct 3 16,000 4 threatened **2** 1 What do all species need? All species need each other. 2 What do people use plants for? To eat, as medicines, and in industry. 3 What does WWF protect? It protects threatened species all around the world. 4 How many insects are there on Earth? There are ten quintillion. **3** 1 protect 2 flowers 3 seeds 4 animals 5 home **4 Example answers** 1 So they can hatch safely on quieter beaches. 2 for meat and for ivory 3 They care for young elephants when their parents have been killed. **5** free answers

Page 50–51 **1** 1 coal 2 Earth 3 oil 4 air 5 land 6 sun 7 wind 8 water **2** 1 Earth has everything that plants and animals need. True 2 People don't damage Earth with pollution. False 3 Too much carbon dioxide is changing Earth's climate. True 4 Some countries are becoming colder and wetter. True 5 People don't need much land to build towns and cities. False **3** 1 environment 2 much 3 chairs, tables 4 electricity 5 recycle **4 Example answers** 1 to make electricity 2 gasoline 3 biogas 4 turn them off 5 We will use fewer fossil fuels. 6 By reusing and recycling things.